SO YOU THINK YOU

Enid Blyton's

The
Famous
Five?

SO YOU THINK YOU KNOW

Enid Blyton's

The
Famous
Five?

WITHDRAWN FROM STOCK

CLIVE GIFFORD

Hodder
Children's
Books

A division of Hachette Children's Books

Text copyright © 2014 Hodder Children's Books
Cover illustration © Hodder & Stoughton Ltd.
Enid Blyton's signature is a Registered Trade Mark of
Hodder & Stoughton Ltd.

First published in Great Britain in 2014 by Hodder Children's Books

A Catalogue record for this book is available from the British Library

ISBN 978 1 444 92166 3

Printed and bound in Great Britain by Clays Ltd, St Ives plc

The paper and board used in this paperback by Hodder Children's Books
are natural recyclable products made from wood grown in sustainable
forests. The manufacturing processes conform to the environmental
regulations of the country of origin.

Hodder Children's Books
A division of Hachette Children's Books
338 Euston Road, London NW1 3BH
An Hachette UK company

www.hodderchildrens.co.uk

Contents

Introduction

So you think you know all about the adventurous world of the Famous Five? Reckon you can recall all the wonderful places they visit, the amazing characters they encounter, the mysteries they solve and the criminals they unmask? Then this is the book for you! Contained within these pages are over a thousand questions on all 21 Famous Five novels as well as the Famous Five short stories and some questions about the author, Enid Blyton. Some are as fun as a picnic on Kirrin Island whilst others are as tricky as the science experiments Uncle Quentin conducts. The questions are divided into 21 quizzes with an easier one to get you started at the beginning and a tougher one at the end as a final test. We hope you find them all an enjoyable challenge.

About the author

Clive Gifford is the award-winning author of over 150 books including the *So You Think You Know* series of quiz books as well as *Teenage Kicks*, *Dead Or Alive*, *Think Again* and *Out Of This World*. His books have been shortlisted for Times Educational Supplement, Royal Society and Blue Peter book awards and have won Smithsonian, NAPPA and School Library Association prizes. Clive lives in Manchester and loves ginger beer.

Easy Questions

1. Which member of the Famous Five is a girl who prefers to be known by a boy's name?

2. How many of the Famous Five are animals?

3. Are there 7, 14 or 21 full-length Famous Five books?

4. Who is the oldest member of the Famous Five?

5. What is the name of the very first Famous Five book?

6. Who is the youngest schoolboy in the Famous Five?

7. Which character, created by Enid Blyton, lives in Toyland and has a friend called Big Ears?

8. What is the name of the island owned by George's family?

9. Which member of the Famous Five is an only child?

10. What is the name of George's mother?

11. Who is the youngest member of the Famous Five?

12. What is the name of the dog in the Famous Five?

13. Enid Blyton's books have sold over 600 million copies: true or false?

14. In *Five Have A Wonderful Time*, whilst staying in Faynights Field, do George and Anne sleep in the blue or the red caravan?

15. What is the name of Aunt Fanny's husband?

16. How many children did Enid Blyton have?

17. What colour is the dog in the Famous Five?

18. How many different families do the Famous Five come from?

19. Three of the Famous Five books are set in mainland Europe: true or false?

20. Which member of Anne's family catches scarlet fever in *Five Go Adventuring Again*?

21. What large animal pulls the front cart in the circus procession the Famous Five watch in *Five Go Off In A Caravan*?

22. Which member of George's family is very forgetful and hot-tempered?

23. What animals do the Famous Five see first on Kirrin Island?

24. Which member of the Famous Five acts as cook on their first caravan holiday?

25. Who has the fiercest temper out of the Famous Five?

26. In *Five Are Together Again*, do the Famous Five camp in a field, stay inside Professor Hayling's house or live in caravans?

27. In *Five On A Hike Together*, Julian tells Anne and George to bring two pairs of what clothing for their hike?

28. Is Quentin a policeman, a secret agent or a scientist?

29. Who helps George make a cardboard collar for Timmy in *Five On A Secret Trail*?

30. What is the name of Mr Henning's son: Henry, Trevor or Junior?

31. Whose father builds a strange tower on Kirrin Island in *Five On Kirrin Island Again*?

32. Which member of the Famous Five wants to fly aeroplanes one day?

33. In *Five On A Treasure Island*, what is the name of the house where George and her parents live?

34. Was Enid Blyton born in 1897, 1927 or 1957?

35. Is Mr Luffy a teacher at Dick and Julian's school, a lodger at Kirrin Cottage or one of Uncle Quentin's scientist friends?

36. Does George, Anne or Joanna mostly dress in boys' clothes?

37. Which two members of the Famous Five go missing in *Five Fall Into Adventure*?

38. In *Five Go To Mystery Moor* which one of the following is not a real horse: Clip, Winkie or Clopper?

39. In *Five On Kirrin Island Again* does the boys' train or the girls' train arrive at Kirrin first at the start of the Easter holidays?

40. Is Mr Roland, the tutor, short and bearded or tall and thin with a drooping moustache?

41. Which member of the Famous Five is put in charge by their parents in *Five Go Off In A Caravan*?

42. In *Five Have A Mystery To Solve*, which member of the Famous Five surprisingly shouts at the men pushing Wilfrid's boat away?

43. In the second Famous Five book, is the new cook at Kirrin Cottage called Joshua, Joanna, Joseph or Jacqueline?

44. Is the tent Anne and George use in *Five On A Secret Trail* waterproof or not?

45. Timmy is a pedigree Alsatian dog: true or false?

46. In the short story *Five Have A Puzzling Time*, which member of the Famous Five has bad toothache?

47. In *Five On A Treasure Island*, what does the storm throw up from the sea: a treasure chest, a shipwreck or an injured dolphin?

48. In *Five Have Plenty Of Fun*, who absent-mindedly spreads mustard instead of marmalade on toast?

49. There has been a Tapper's Circus held in the field next to Professor Hayling's house for over 350 years: true or false?

50. Enid Blyton is said to have based one character from the Famous Five on herself. Who is it?

Medium Questions

1. Which member of the Famous Five really dislikes mustard: Julian, Anne or George?

2. How much money does Uncle Quentin give the children for getting good reports at school: 25p, £1.00 or £10.00?

3. Is Professor Hayling's house found at Big Hollow, Great Giddings, Demon's Cave or Beckton?

4. Enid Blyton was born at 354 Lordship Lane. Did she write more books than this house number?

5. From which country does Mr Jenkins, the gardener at Dick, Julian and Anne's home, come?

6. Does Kirrin Island contain a small village, a ruined castle or a harbour and inn?

7. Was the first known published work by Enid Blyton a children's story, a sports report or a poem?

8. Who, in the second Famous Five book, has never seen a pantomime or circus before?

9. Who is the owner of the travelling fair in *Five Have Plenty Of Fun*: the Guv'nor, Red Tower or Gringo?

10. In which book do Anne and George go to a riding school for a week: *Five Get Into A Fix*, *Five Run Away Together* or *Five Go To Mystery Moor*?

11. In which book do the Famous Five meet the twins called 'the two Harries'?

12. What is the name of Guy Lawdler's dog: Sooty, Jet, Blackie or Midnight?

13. In *Five Have A Mystery To Solve*, who asks the Famous Five to look after her grandson in her house?

14. Which rude American child throws a bun on the kitchen floor for Timmy at Finniston Farm: Berta, Junior or Scott?

15. In *Five On A Treasure Island*, which adult takes the box from the shipwreck away from the Famous Five?

16. In *Five Go Off To Camp*, which friendly adult camps close to the Famous Five: Mr Reynolds, Mr Luffy or Mr Andrews?

17. Who has a puncture to the rear tyre of their bicycle at the very start of *Five Go Down To The Sea*?

18. What is the name of the lake the Five swim in near the start of *Five Get Into Trouble*: Kirrin Lake, the Green Pool or Wilderness Lake?

19. In *Five Go To Billycock Hill*, which member of the Five shakes hands first with Binky the dog?

20. Which boat do the Five choose to hire in *Five Have A Mystery To Solve*: Rock-A-Bye, Starfish, Adventure or Endeavour?

21. Who is Mr Gringle's business partner: Ray Wells, Mr Brent or Mr Thomas?

22. In *Five Get Into A Fix*, who is the first member of the Famous Five to awake on their first morning in Magga Glen farmhouse?

23. Is Mr Stick a travelling salesman, a sailor or a farmer?

24. Which of the Five do the others have to hide at Smuggler's Top?

25. In which book do the Famous Five find packages of hundred-dollar banknotes?

26. Is the kitchen-maid at Smuggler's Top called Harriet, Sarah or Marybelle?

27. Which member of the Famous Five suggests the idea of a caravanning holiday in *Five Go Off In A Caravan*?

28. Is a horse that pulled one of the Famous Five's caravans called: Trotter, Black Queen or Old Lady?

29. In which book do the Famous Five stay in a lighthouse and visit Wreckers' Cave?

30. At the start of *Five On A Hike Together*, which of the Famous Five writes to Anne?

31. Which member of the fair folk in Faynights Field is a knife thrower and can perform rope tricks?

32. In *Five Go To Demon's Rocks*, what sort of creature is Mischief: a dog, a weasel, a monkey or a tabby cat?

33. How many dogs do the owners of Tremannon Farm have?

34. What disease is Joanna the cook suffering from in *Five Are Together Again*: measles, scarlet fever, typhoid or malaria?

35. With which girl at the riding school does George constantly argue and bicker?

36. In *Five Have Plenty Of Fun*, is Berta, the American girl, staying at Kirrin Cottage because her father: is ill, has gone missing or fears she might be kidnapped?

37. Which schoolfriend of Dick's tells him about a butterfly farm at Billycock Hill?

38. In which month of the year do the events in *Five On A Secret Trail* occur?

39. Which member of the Famous Five is locked in a bedroom at Smuggler's Top with just bread and water as punishment?

40. What creature does Wilfrid pull out of his pocket and scare Anne with when they first meet?

41. What do the Famous Five use to mark their way through the dungeons of Kirrin Castle?

42. Which boy does George slap on the cheek in anger at the start of *Five Run Away Together*?

43. In *Good Old Timmy!* who is the boy the Famous Five make friends with: Harold, Oliver or Billy?

44. In *Five On Kirrin Island Again*, what is the first meal the Famous Five and Aunt Fanny have on Kirrin Island: breakfast, lunch, tea or supper?

45. Who lives at Spiggy House: Mr Roland, Mr Gaston or Jim Willis?

46. Does Jeremiah Boogle, One-Ear Bill or Ebenezer hide the wreckers' treasure?

47. Which member of Sniffer's family wears large gold earrings: his father, his brother or his sister?

48. Which member of the Famous Five is not allowed into Faynights Castle but manages to find a way in?

49. What is the name of the girl dressed only in shirt and shorts found by Dick and Julian on the snowy mountain in *Five Get Into A Fix*?

50. As a schoolgirl, Enid Blyton was captain of which sports team?

QUIZ 2

1. Which of the Famous Five is teased for wearing a ponytail because of the heat, at the start of *Five On Finniston Farm*?

2. How old is Julian at the start of *Five On A Treasure Island*?

3. In which British city was Enid Blyton born: London, Manchester or Edinburgh?

4.   Who is the only member of the Famous Five not ill on Christmas Day in *Five Get Into A Fix*?

5.   In which book do the Famous Five stay in caravans in the grounds of Faynights Castle?

6.   What is the name of Sniffer's dog: Tommy, Liz, Barker or Meg?

7.   What is the name of the circus boy the Famous Five meet at the start of *Five Go Off In A Caravan*: Benny, Billy, Nobby or Davey?

8.   How many towers does the ruined castle on Kirrin Island have?

9.   In *Five Go Adventuring Again*, does Aunt Fanny transport Anne and George from the train station to Kirrin Cottage in a pony trap, an old car or a horse and cart?

10.   In which room in Kirrin Cottage does George discover eight wooden panels?

11.   In *Five Run Away Together*, is Tinker a boat repairer, a dog, a fisherman or a lodger at Kirrin Farmhouse?

12. In which book do the Famous Five first go on a cycling and camping trip?

13. Which place in Cornwall are the Famous Five heading to at the start of *Five Go Down To The Sea*: Porthleven, St Ives, Tremannon or Polperro?

14. What is the name of the boy who lives in Hill Cottage and has many wild animals as friends: Cyril, Harry, Wilfrid or Bobby?

15. Which two of the Famous Five do not climb up out of the well to escape the treasure room in *Five Have A Mystery To Solve*?

16. In *Five Get Into Trouble*, who has to be at conferences during the Easter holidays: Uncle Quentin, Julian's father or Aunt Fanny?

17. Anne names one of the puppies at Olly's Farm: Tickles, Cuddles or Hugs?

18. Does the tree crash through the attic, the kitchen or lounge of Kirrin Cottage in *Five Go To Smuggler's Top*?

19. In which month of the year is *Five On Kirrin Island Again* set?

20. What gardening tool does Bobby Loman use as an oar when rowing to Kirrin Island?

21. Is Anne and George's school house mistress called Mrs Johnson, Miss Peters, Mrs Benson or Miss Harris?

22. Is Billycock Hill shaped like a bird, an old-fashioned hat or a tall stone tower?

23. Who ties a bright blue ribbon to Timmy's tail when he, George and Anne explore the ruined cottage in *Five On A Secret Trail*?

24. Which member of the Famous Five finds Jet the dog behind the fallen rocks underground?

25. Is the American girl who joins the Famous Five in *Five Have Plenty Of Fun* called Jackie, Berta, Wilma or Hattie?

26. What is inside the parcels dropped by aeroplane on to Mystery Moor and the quarry?

27. Does Dick, Julian or George report the burglary at Demon's Rocks lighthouse to the police?

28. Is Pearl, Dacca or Anita a tap dancer in *Five Have A Wonderful Time*?

29. Does Mr Wooh, the Boneless Man or Mr Tapper have only one ear?

30. In *Five Go To Demon's Rocks*, what is Tinker Hayling mad keen on: cars, fierce animals, aeroplanes or battles and castles?

31. What relation is Mr Lenoir to Pierre Lenoir: father, stepfather, uncle or cousin?

32. On their first visit to Wreckers' Cave, who finds a gold coin: Mischief, Tinker, Julian or Anne?

33. Which boy in *Five Get Into Trouble*, who the Famous Five think is a coward and liar, turns into a hero at the end?

34. In *Five Fall Into Adventure*, in what vehicle do Red and Markhoff plan to escape?

35. How many floors does the farmhouse at Finniston Farm have?

36. What is the name of Toby Thomas's little brother: George, Billy, David or Benny?

37. What is the name of the strange building the Famous Five find padlocked on their way to Magga Glen in *Five Get Into A Fix*?

38. In *Five Fall Into Adventure*, does Jo the ragamuffin live in a tent, a small shack or a caravan?

39. Is one of the two men threatening to blow up Kirrin Island called Johnson, Chapman, Dickinson or Simpson?

40. What colour are the wheels of Nobby's caravan painted?

41. Is *Merry Meg, Saucy Jane* or *Careful Carrie* the first boat the Famous Five discover on Gloomy Lake?

42. Which of the Famous Five is angry at Berta sleeping in their room?

43. What sport does Charlie the chimpanzee thrill the Famous Five by playing in *Five Are Together Again*?

44. Does Jock, Wooden-Leg Sam, Cecil or Mr Andrews throw cinders at the Famous Five in *Five Go Off To Camp*?

45. Does Mr Binks, George Roth or the Guv'nor turn out to be a smuggler in *Five Go Down To The Sea*?

46. In *Five Run Away Together*, which boy sings nasty songs about George at Kirrin Cottage?

47. At Demon's Rocks, who stays to guard the lighthouse after the burglary: Julian, Timmy, Dick or George?

48. Was Hugh Alexander Pollock Enid Blyton's husband, father or son?

49. In *Five On Finniston Farm*, Mr Henning comes from which country?

50. At Billycock Farm, Toby Thomas's little brother has a pet pig. Is its name Pinky, Curly, Porky or Binky?

1. Which member of the Famous Five is kidnapped by mistake in *Five Get Into Trouble*?

2. At the start of *Five Go Off In A Caravan*, do the Famous Five see a town parade, a circus procession or a troop of marching soldiers?

3. What is the name of the family who lives at Finniston Farm: Henning, Philpot, Finniston or Durleston?

4. Who once poured custard all over his fish dinner by mistake: Dick, Uncle Quentin, Sniffer or Julian?

5. What was Enid Blyton's middle name: Joanna, Mary, Berta or Clare?

6. In which month does *Five Have A Wonderful Time* start?

7. In *Five Have Plenty Of Fun*, does Berta have blue, green or brown eyes?

8. Do George and Anne play Snap, the Alphabet game or Happy Families to pass the time in the old, ruined cottage in *Five On A Secret Trail*?

9. How many extra days' half term holiday do Julian and Dick get in *Five On A Hike Together*?

10. Who lives at Kirrin Farm: the Sanders, the Jacksons or the Rolands?

11. Is *Five Run Away Together* set in summer, in winter or in the Easter holidays?

12. Is Mr Penruthlan a scientist, a farmer, a fisherman or a policeman?

13. In *Five Go Off To Camp*, who is furious that Dick, Julian and Jock went to spy on the spook trains without asking them?

14. What is the name of the riding school in *Five Go To Mystery Moor*?

15. Was coal, marble, sand or gravel originally mined at the quarry on Mystery Moor?

16. In *Five Go To Billycock Hill*, Toby upsets Anne and George with what joke creature?

17. In *Five On A Secret Trail*, is it Tom, Guy or Paul who steals the blueprints?

18. Is Red Tower a real place, a person or a pretend place that Joanna the cook talks about?

19. How do people get to the top of Uncle Quentin's tower on Kirrin Island: by a lift, a spiral staircase or a cable car?

20. In *Five Fall Into Adventure*, have Julian, Dick and Anne just spent six weeks in Spain, France or Italy?

21. Do Richard Kent and the Famous Five have tea together in Great Giddings, Middlecombe Woods or Croker's Corner?

22. Who pushes Mr Wooh into the sea: George, Timmy or Julian?

23. In *Five On Kirrin Island Again*, which member of the Famous Five describes Uncle Quentin as a 'wet blanket'?

24. Is Mr Luffy a poor swimmer or a good swimmer?

25. At the start of *Five Go To Demon's Rocks*, are Dick, Julian and Anne's parents going on a walking holiday, a cruise or a sightseeing trip to Rome?

26. In the short story *Five Have A Puzzling Time*, what colour are Anne's sandals?

27. Which part of his body does Timmy injure when chasing rabbits down a rabbit hole in *Five On A Hike Together*?

28. In *Five Run Away Together*, what colour is George's boat painted?

29. Do the Famous Five take a portable radio, a petrol generator or an electric heater with them on their trip to Billycock Hill?

30. In *Five Go Down To The Sea*, is Janie Coster a fiddle player, an old-time dancer or a comedian?

31. Which member of the Famous Five wins a small ball at the fair's hoopla stall in *Five Have Plenty Of Fun*?

32. What sort of tree falls on Kirrin Cottage in *Five Go To Smuggler's Top*?

33. Does Julian, Dick, George or Wilfrid manage to remove the ball from Timmy's throat in *Five Have A Mystery To Solve*?

34. In *Five Go Off To Camp*, how do the Famous Five travel to their campsite on the moors: by boat, train, car or bicycle?

35. In *Five Go To Billycock Hill* do the Five see a six-spot day-flying butterfly, moth or secret aircraft?

36. Are the names of the two criminals in the short story *A Lazy Afternoon*: Bill and Jack, Jim and Stan or Reg and Dave?

37. What animal do Sid and Mr Binks say they're going to replace their horse costume with?

38. In *Five Go To Mystery Moor*, what sound wakes the Famous Five up on their first night of camping?

39. In *Five Get Into A Fix*, who writes a note saying her son has been killed and she is being held prisoner in her own house?

40. At the end of *Five Go Down To The Sea*, which member of the Famous Five cooks hard-boiled eggs as their part in making tea?

41. In *Five Go To Demon's Rocks*, is the new lighthouse built at Wreckers' Cove, Salty Rocks or High Cliffs?

42. What name, beginning with the letter T, does Professor Hayling say his son is called?

43. What is the name of the school that Anne and George attend: Gaylands, Oaktree or St Ruth's?

44. Which member of the Famous Five is slightly injured by a thorn while out on Mystery Moor?

45. Which of the Famous Five figures out the dog thieves' plan in the short story *Five And A Half-Term Adventure*?

46. In which year was the Famous Five Club formed for fans of the series: 1952, 1972 or 1992?

47. Is Alfredo a snake handler, a trapeze artist or a fire eater?

48. Are Julian and Dick in France, Scotland, Spain or Ireland when Anne arrives at Kirrin Cottage in *Five On A Secret Trail*?

49. In which book does Mrs Stick first appear?

50. Who do the Famous Five call 'Spotty-Face': Mr Roland, Edgar Stick or Sooty Lenoir?

QUIZ 4

1. In *Five On A Secret Trail*, which member of the Famous Five comes out in spots during a trip to France?

2. Is Smuggler's Top surrounded by marshes, rocky mountains or the water of a lake?

3. Is Mr Luffy a very slow driver, a very fast driver or a non-driver?

4. Does George take Dick, Julian and Anne to Kirrin Island for the very first time using a rowing boat, motor-boat or pair of canoes?

5. In which book do the Famous Five investigate 'spook trains' and meet Jock Robins?

6.   In which month of the year is *Five On A Hike Together* set?

7.   What type of birds peck at a baby rabbit in the short story *Five Have A Puzzling Time*: eagles, ravens, jackdaws or seagulls?

8.   What is the name of the thin little traveller boy who brings an injured horse to Captain Johnson for treatment?

9.   Who lies to Red that he has smashed up George's boat in *Five Fall Into Adventure*: Simmy, Markhoff, Jake or Rooky?

10. What is the name of the lady who cooks at Owl Dene: Jennie, Aggie, Gemma or Constance?

11. Which member of the Famous Five first travels through the tunnel under the sea in Kirrin Bay?

12. In *Five On Kirrin Island Again*, when the Famous Five meet for their Easter holidays, do they eat eggs and bacon, ham sandwiches or buns at the train station?

13. Is Dick, Toby, Jeff or Mr Gringle fond of practical jokes, with a fake flower that squirts water?

14. In which book does Mrs Daly first appear: *Five Run Away Together*, *Five Go To Smuggler's Top* or *Five Get Into A Fix*?

15. What is the name of the wealthy smuggler who lives on Castaway Hill: Chambers, Barling or Davidson?

16. In *Five Go Off To Camp*, is the watchman who lives next to the train line missing an eye, an arm or a leg?

17. How many floors are shown on the old map of Kirrin Castle the cousins find in *Five On A Treasure Island*?

18. In what month is the short story *Five And A Half-Term Adventure* set?

19. Is Uncle Dan, Lou, Larry or Rossy the chief clown of the circus in *Five Go Off In A Caravan*?

20. Which member of the Famous Five is hurt at the start of *Five On A Secret Trail*?

21. In *Five Fall Into Adventure*, what creatures do the Famous Five encounter when walking through the caves towards Red's house?

22. Enid Blyton's Malory Towers series was based on a boarding school in which English county: Lancashire, Cornwall or Sussex?

23. Is Milling Green, Tremannon or Great Giddings the nearest bus stop to Captain Johnson's Riding School?

24. In *Five Have A Wonderful Time*, who insists on sleeping underneath George and Anne's caravan?

25. Where does Julian find the controls to open a secret room in Owl Dene: in a bookcase, underneath a desk or behind a curtain?

26. Is Anita, Joanna or Skippy a good guitar player and the wife of Bufflo?

27. Do the Famous Five stop for lunch at Fallaway Hill, Croker's Cross or Coney Copse on the first day of their walk in *Five On A Hike Together*?

28. What is the real name of the boy at Finniston Farm nicknamed 'Harry'?

29. In *Five Have Plenty Of Fun*, does James, Joanna, Uncle Quentin or Mr Roland fix the rowlock on George's boat?

30. In *Five Have A Wonderful Time*, had naughty children let out snakes, canaries or performing dogs from their cages the last time the fair visited?

31. What amazing present had Tinker received on his last birthday in *Five Go To Demon's Rocks*?

32. In *Five Go Down To The Sea*, what is being smuggled: diamonds, gold bars, dangerous drugs or old paintings?

33. Are the Famous Five off school for one week, three weeks or six weeks in *Five Go To Billycock Hill*?

34. In *Five Run Away Together*, who stops working at Kirrin Cottage to go and nurse her mother who has a broken leg?

35. Does Mrs Layman live in Rose Mansions, Cliff Villas or Hill Cottage?

36. Which two of the Five get inside the donkey costume owned by Tappin's Circus?

37. Who is the housekeeper at Big Hollow: Joanna, Jacqueline, Jenny or Josephine?

38. Does Tinker, George or Dick have a fight with Jeremy the circus boy in *Five Are Together Again*?

39. In *Five Get Into A Fix*, how many dogs are there at Magga Glen farm?

40. Is Mrs Stick a doll, a cook, a teacher or a policewoman?

41. Whose bike does Jo take to follow Dick, Julian and Timmy in *Five Have Plenty Of Fun*?

42. How many miles is Tremannon Farm from Polwilly Halt: four, eight or sixteen?

43. In *Five Run Away Together*, is Jennifer Armstrong's middle name Mary, Hattie or Bella?

44. To which country do the Famous Five go on holiday in *Five Get Into A Fix*?

45. Who is the last of the Famous Five to leave the treasure room on Whispering Island, crashing a table down next to one of the men?

46. Does Bill, Henry or Trevor drive the Famous Five around Finniston Farm in an old Land Rover?

47. Which of the Famous Five discovers the trunk on the shipwreck in *Five Run Away Together*?

48. What is the name of the elephant the Famous Five encounter at the circus?

49. In *Five Run Away Together*, do the Five use heather, duvets, or inflatable cushions as beds in their cave?

50. What happens to the aeroplanes stolen from Billycock Hill airfield: are they are flown to Belgium, do they crash into the sea or are they quickly recovered?

1. At the start of *Five Have A Wonderful Time*, which member of the Famous Five has a week in bed with a bad cold?

2. In 1913, Enid Blyton had her first foreign holiday. To which country did she travel?

3. In *Five Go Off To Camp*, who has brown eyes, hairs growing out of his nose and can waggle his ear?

4. What colour hair does the kidnapped girl have in *Five Run Away Together*?

5. In *Five Have Plenty Of Fun*, which character found in earlier books now lives with Joanna the cook's cousin?

6. In *Five On Kirrin Island Again*, has Mr Curton built his own glider, radio transmitter or television?

7. What sort of creature is Pongo: a skunk, a chimpanzee, a dog or an elephant?

8. Does Mr Roland buy George, Julian or Uncle Quentin a book about dogs for Christmas?

9. In *Five Go To Mystery Moor*, what does Henrietta only let her very best friends call her: Henry, Harry or Etta?

10. Which one of the following is not a child staying at Captain Johnson's Riding School: Amanda, Rita, William or George?

11. Which adult spills ink over a set of very important blueprints in *Five On A Secret Trail*?

12. In which book do we meet Tinker and his father, Professor Hayling, for a second time?

13. Who makes Anne so angry in *Five Have A Mystery To Solve* that she throws a bucket of cold water over them?

14. In *Five Go Off In A Caravan*, do the Famous Five start their holidays at home, at Kirrin Cottage or at Smuggler's Top?

15. Are most of the dogs at Tremannon Farm terriers, collies or German shepherds?

16. Is Faynights Castle home to lots of seagulls, ravens, jackdaws or eagles?

17. In *Five Fall Into Adventure*, are Aunt Fanny and Uncle Quentin off on a tour of Germany, Italy, Spain or Canada?

18. Who makes Timmy the dog his own sandwiches at the start of *Five Get Into Trouble*: George, Anne or Aunt Fanny?

19. In *Five On Kirrin Island Again*, which person won't go down into the dungeons to look for Uncle Quentin?

20. Is Tinker Hayling younger or older than Anne?

21. Which boat found in the boathouse on Gloomy Lake has a boy's name beginning with the letter C?

22. Do Julian, Dick, Anne and Sid play Monopoly, Snap or marbles in *Five Fall Into Adventure*?

23. Which boy in *Five Get Into Trouble* has already had two bikes stolen before he meets the Famous Five?

24. What is the nickname of Mrs Taggart's son, part of which is the same as the name of one of the Famous Five?

25. Which character steals a bone from Timmy's bowl in *Five Go To Demon's Rocks*?

26. What is the first winter sport or pastime the Famous Five play in *Five Get Into A Fix*: snowballing, tobogganing, skiing or snowboarding?

27. As a young man, did Enid Blyton's father sell cars, cutlery or fine wines to make a living?

28. What is the name of Mrs Jones's enormous and strong son: Henry, Dai, Ewan or Morgan?

29. What fruit do Julian and Dick pick from the garden of Kirrin Cottage to take with them on their very first visit to Kirrin Island?

30. Is Jim, Reg, Peter or David the boatman repainting George's boat in *Five Run Away Together*?

31. Does Julian describe scientists, aircraft pilots, policemen or doctors as very important people in *Five On Kirrin Island Again*?

32. Does Timmy bite a man called Block on the arm, leg or head the day before Uncle Quentin arrives at Smuggler's Top?

33. In *Five Get Into A Fix*, who races on the toboggan along with Julian?

34. Does old Mrs Thomas live in Old Towers, the watermill or Magga Glen farmhouse?

35. Does George get locked in an iron-mongers shop, a hairdressers or a pet shop during a robbery in the short story *George's Hair Is Too Long*?

36. In *Five Go To Billycock Hill*, is Toby's cousin Jeff a scientist, a burglar, an air force pilot or a farmer?

37. In *Five Have Plenty Of Fun*, how does Berta reach England: by plane, boat, rail or hot air balloon?

38. What is the first meal the Famous Five enjoy at Big Hollow: sausages and mash, roast pork, stew or spaghetti?

39. When the Famous Five arrive at Billycock Farm, is the first meal Mrs Thomas serves them breakfast, lunch, tea or supper?

40. In *Five Have A Wonderful Time*, to which British city does Uncle Quentin travel in order to prove that Derek Terry-Kane is not a traitor?

41. Can you name either of the performing dogs that the Famous Five meet at the start of *Five Go Off In A Caravan*?

42. Does Aunt Fanny make everyone ginger beer, tea, hot cocoa or milky coffee after a tree crashes on to Kirrin Cottage?

43. What do the Famous Five buy Jeremiah Boogle in return for him telling them his stories?

44. What name is given to the people who lured ships on to the rocks in Cornwall to shipwreck them and steal their cargo?

45. Does Tinker, Mischief or Dick blow PC Sharp's whistle at the end of *Five Go To Demon's Rocks*?

46. Which of the Five suffers a bad cut to the head on Mystery Moor?

47. In *Five Go Adventuring Again*, are the children to get three, five or seven hours of schoolwork with their tutor each day?

48. Is Slider, Beauty or Emerald the name of the python snake that follows Jo into the tower of Faynights Castle?

49. In *Five On Kirrin Island Again*, who suggests going to the old quarry to look for prehistoric weapons?

50. Which of the Five sinks in the marshes surrounding Smuggler's Top and has to be rescued?

QUIZ 6

1. At what speed is Julian supposed to warn Mr Luffy to drive more slowly: 35, 55 or 75 miles per hour?

2. What is the name of the old horse Julian, Dick and Anne's family keep in the field next to their home?

3. Which scientist's important papers are ransacked in *Five Are Together Again*?

4. Mr Tapper tells Tinker that he has a licence to hold the circus in the field once every: year, five years or ten years?

5. At the start of her writing career, did Enid Blyton write out her books by hand, use a typewriter or dictate the stories to her secretary?

6. What was the name of the travelling fair Jo had visited in *Five Have Plenty Of Fun*?

7. In *Five Go Down To The Sea*, is Edith Wells, George Roth or Janie Coster advertised as 'The nightingale singer'?

8. What was the name of the family who built the railway line on Mystery Moor: Startle, Bartle or Battle?

9. Which of the Famous Five is nearly blown over the lighthouse railings and into the sea when trying to hit a warning bell?

10. What animal do the Famous Five spot on Kirrin Island that leads them to meet Bobby Loman and his dog: a dolphin, a horse or a monkey?

11. In *Five On Finniston Farm*, does Mr Durleston say Lady Phillippa has four, eight or fifteen children?

12. What colour eyes does George have?

13. Who is so ill they have to be taken to hospital in *Five Run Away Together*: Uncle Quentin, Dick, Aunt Fanny or Mr Sanders?

14. What type of dog is Chummy: a Labrador, an Alsatian or a cocker spaniel?

15. Do the Famous Five travel from Kirrin Cottage to Smuggler's Top by car, yacht, coach or paddle-steamer?

16. In which book do the Famous Five encounter a circus and foil robbers?

17. Which dog is poisoned by meat placed next to the caravans by the circus men: Timmy, Barker or Growler?

18. In *Five On Kirrin Island Again*, who does Mr Curton pretend is his son: James, Michael, Jack or Martin?

19. In *Five On Kirrin Island Again*, are Uncle Quentin's great experiments about space rockets a new way of generating power or time travel?

20. Which member of the Famous Five thinks the smoke from the hills is a volcano in *Five Go Off To Camp*?

21. In *Five Get Into Trouble*, how much does Mr Perton give the Five as an apology for kidnapping Dick?

22. In *Five Fall Into Adventure*, does Sid, Jake or Julian pay Jo to help perform crimes?

23. Was Enid Blyton's youngest brother named Colin, Clive, Carey or Charles?

24. In *Five On A Treasure Island*, do the children's parents head off to Scotland, France or Spain on holiday?

25. When Dick and Jo have a contest in *Five Fall Into Adventure*, are they: throwing a pebble, spitting a damson stone or kicking a ball?

26. Does the policeman in Reebles believe the Famous Five's story about the prisoner and the strange message Dick receives?

27. What is the name of the lake high on the moors in *Five On A Hike Together*?

28. Do the Famous Five meet a rubber man and a snake handler in *Five Have A Wonderful Time*, *Five Run Away Together* or *Five Go Off To Camp*?

29. Does it cost 5p, 25p or 50p to enter Faynights Castle?

30. What is the reason that Mr Penruthlan always mumbles words the Famous Five can't understand at dinner time?

31. Was the last Noddy book Enid Blyton wrote: *Noddy Goes To Sea*, *Noddy And The Aeroplane* or *Noddy And Tessie Bear*?

32. Does the suspicious Mr Curton tell Dick that he works as a private investigator, spy, scientist or journalist?

33. In which holiday is *Five Go To Smuggler's Top* set, is it: Easter, Christmas or in the summer holidays?

34. Which member of the circus does Nobby live with, in a caravan?

35. How many stories are contained in the book called *The Famous Five Short Story Collection*?

36. According to Ben the blacksmith, what happened to all the Bartles: they were arrested by police, they moved abroad or they vanished on the moor?

37. At the start of *Five Have Plenty Of Fun*, which member of the Famous Five is given a pound coin by an American scientist?

38. Which two of the Five have sardines with bread and butter for breakfast in *Five On A Secret Trail*?

39. As they head to Billycock Caves, who tells the other members of the Famous Five that stalactites grow from the cave roof downwards?

40. At the start of *Five Have A Wonderful Time* do the fair folk welcome the Famous Five, ignore them or tell them to clear off and leave the field?

41. Are George and Timmy held as prisoners in a caravan in Middlecombe Woods, Demon's Cove or Ravens Wood?

42. Does Dick, Martin, Anne or Julian twist their ankle climbing around the old quarry in *Five On Kirrin Island Again*?

43. What breed is the Harries' dog, Snippet: Labrador, poodle, red setter or Alsatian?

44. Which one of the following is not a landmark on Finniston Farm: Hangman's Copse, Oak Tree Pond or Tinker's Wood?

45. In *Five Go To Demon's Rocks*, how do people reach the top of the lighthouse: by lift, by a spiral staircase or by climbing up on ropes?

46. On the circus posters in *Five Are Together Again*, who is billed as 'The Wonder Wizard'?

47. In which book do the Famous Five stay in a hut on the side of a Welsh mountain?

48. In *Five On A Secret Trail*, when George and Anne first meet Guy Lawdler, what kind of old coin does he show them?

49. What creature does Wilfrid name Spiky in *Five Have A Mystery To Solve*?

50. On their first visit to Kirrin Island with Berta, who were the two men the Five found walking on the beach?

QUIZ 7

1. When the children set off on their cycling holiday in *Five Get Into Trouble*, who is the only one not wearing shorts?

2. Was Finniston Castle burnt down in 1192, 1324 or 1546?

3. Is Spiky, Sniffer or Jack the boy in charge of the roundabout at Gringo's Great Fair?

4. Which part of the house at Big Hollow does Professor Hayling forbid the Famous Five to go into: the tower, the barn, the library or the kitchen?

5. Which actress played Enid Blyton in the 2009 BBC film about her life: Julie Walters, Judi Dench or Helena Bonham Carter?

6. In the short story *When Timmy Chased The Cat*, what part of her body does the old lady injure when she slips and falls?

7. Is Pierre Lenoir's mother, sister or the Lenoir family cook named Sarah?

8. In *Five Go To Smuggler's Top*, what choice does Uncle Quentin give the children other than to go and stay at Smuggler's Top?

9. In *Five On A Treasure Island*, on what day of the week do the children leave home for Kirrin Island?

10. In which village does Bobby Loman live?

11. Are the walls of Nobby's caravan painted orange and red, purple and green or yellow and blue?

12. In *Five Run Away Together*, which adult says they will phone Kirrin Cottage every day at nine o'clock?

13. In *Five Get Into Trouble*, is the first village the children stop in called Manlington-Tovey, Little Stoddington or Great Giddings?

14. What type of creatures had left their cages and were running through the circus until their handler, Lucilla, returned?

15. At the very start of *Five Get Into A Fix*, who declares the current Christmas holidays the worst he's ever known?

16. In *Five On A Secret Trail*, who finds the blueprints in the leather bag by slitting open the bottom of the bag's lining?

17. Which member of the Famous Five pretends to go into town on the bus but creeps back to where the caravans are parked?

18. Can you name two of the dogs at Tremannon Farm?

19. In *Five Go To Demon's Rocks*, when shopping for food supplies in Kirrin, Julian spends all his money: who does he tell to buy the next batch of food?

20. What is the name of the circus that sets up in the same field as the Famous Five and Tinker planned to camp in?

21. Enid Blyton met her future husband when they were both working on a book about which zoo?

22. Which two of the following items do the Famous Five find on Kirrin Island in the short story *Five Have A Puzzling Time*: dog biscuits, sardine sandwiches, orange peel, an empty box of chocolates?

23. In *Five On Kirrin Island Again*, do the men planning to steal Uncle Quentin's secrets reach Kirrin Island by yacht, submarine, parachute or hot air balloon?

24. Whose mother is Mrs Stick: Edgar's, Jo's, Tinker's or Martin's?

25. Is *Five Have A Mystery To Solve* set in April, July, August or October?

26. Where does Timmy hide all the Christmas presents he recovers from the thief in Kirrin?

27. What do the Famous Five use to travel from their mountain hut to the slopes of the hill on which Old Towers stands?

28. What is the name of the farm close to where the Five camp in *Five Go Off To Camp*: Olly's Farm, Longworth Farm or Skipper's Farm?

29. Which two characters meet Julian, Dick and Anne at the train station right at the start of *Five Fall Into Adventure*?

30. Which of the Five receives a strange message whilst staying at Mrs Taggart's house?

31. What type of snake do the Five first see come out of Mr Slither's box when he arrives next to their caravans: a rattlesnake, a cobra or a python?

32. Do Dick and Julian spy Mr Binks, Yan's great-grandfather or Mr Penruthlan going through the pockets of the Barnies' clothes and costumes in the barn?

33. Does Sniffer, William or Henrietta have a very loud snore which keeps George awake?

34. How do the Famous Five learn about the theft of aircraft from Billycock Hill: does Mr Gringle tell them, do they read it in the newspaper or do they hear it on the radio?

35. Who confirms that the blueprints found in *Five On A Secret Trail* are important scientific plans: the Inspector, Julian, Uncle Quentin or Harry Lawdler?

36. What do the Five buy as a present for Bill in return for the Land Rover ride: a pocket-knife, six macaroons, a new hat or a chocolate cake?

37. In *Five Go To Demon's Rocks*, is the name of Jeremiah's grand-daughter: Jenny, Berta, Millie or Hilary?

38. Are Henrietta's great-aunts, who come to take her out when the others go camping on Mystery Moor, called Hermione and Louisa or Hannah and Lucy?

39. In *Five Go To Billycock Hill*, what sort of dog is Binky: a Labrador, a collie or an Alsatian?

40. What make is the car that carries Mr Perton, Rooky and the other men in *Five Get Into Trouble*: Wolsey, Bentley, Rolls Royce or Daimler?

41. Who shows the Famous Five a secret way into the grounds of Old Towers in *Five Get Into A Fix*: Aily, Morgan or the shepherd?

42. In *Five Get Into A Fix*, what hot drink do the Five give the shepherd on his first visit to the Welsh mountain hut they are staying in?

43. In which book do Julian and Dick get extra holidays as a result of other boys getting scholarships?

44. What is the first name, beginning with the letter E, of Berta's father?

45. In *Five On Kirrin Island Again*, is Benson, Peters, Cooper or Hobbs one of the two men threatening to blow up Kirrin Island?

46. In *Five Go Off To Camp*, what animals cause Mr Luffy to brake sharply on the way to the campsite?

47. What drink does the golf pro give the Five in return for the golf balls Timmy finds: orangeade, ginger beer or lemonade?

48. What is the name of the guard at Kirrin train station who welcomes George and the others in *Five Are Together Again*?

49. What colour are the curtains in the red caravan in *Five Go Off In A Caravan*?

50. Is Georgina, Dick or Julian the first to speak in the very first Famous Five book?

QUIZ 8

1. What is the name of the clever chimpanzee at Tapper's Travelling Circus: Lucky, Charlie, Bananas or Chester?

2. Which person at Smuggler's Top appears to be deaf: Mrs Lenoir, Sarah, Marybelle or Block?

3. Is the lighthouse on Demon's Rocks about 20, 50 or 100 miles west of Kirrin Cottage?

4. Who phones Aunt Fanny in *Five Have A Wonderful Time* to check that Uncle Quentin hasn't disappeared?

5. Is Aily's dog called Rhodri, Dai, Megan or Aled?

6. What are the first treasures the Famous Five see when they go down the well in *Five Have A Mystery To Solve*?

7. Which two boys does Will Janes catch and hold, one in each hand, in *Five Go To Billycock Hill*?

8. What creatures is Mr Luffy most interested in: dogs, insects, fish or birds?

9. What series written by Enid Blyton featured four runaway children called Mike, Peggy, Nora and Jack?

10. What number plane does Jeff fly from the airfield near Billycock Hill: 127, 569, 812 or 973?

11. What pet does Professor Hayling's son bring with him to Kirrin Cottage in *Five Go To Demon's Rocks*?

12. What food does Julian give George on the beach on the very first day they meet in the first book?

13. Does Mrs Penruthlan at Tremannon Farm make huge meals, small meals or no meals at all for the Famous Five?

14. In *Five Run Away Together*, do the children live in a cave, the castle or the shipwreck whilst staying on Kirrin Island?

15. What cargo is the lorry delivering that transports Uncle Quentin, Sooty and the Famous Five from the marshes back to Smuggler's Top?

16. When Pongo first visits the Five's caravans does he steal a torch, sweets, a bottle of ginger beer or an almond cake?

17. Which adult plays a game of Scrabble with the Famous Five in *Five Are Together Again*: Joanna, Jenny or Aunt Fanny?

18. Which character in *Five Go Off In A Caravan* has never turned on a water tap in their life?

19. Is there a glass room, a massive radio transmitter or a powerful laser at the top of Uncle Quentin's tower on Kirrin Island?

20. In *Five Go Off to Camp*, what is the name of the collie dog who has given birth to puppies?

21. Is Anne, George or Richard Kent hiding up a tree when Dick is kidnapped in *Five Get Into Trouble*?

22. Which of the boats does Dirty Dick row from the boathouse on to Gloomy Lake: *Careful Carrie*, *Merry Meg* or *Saucy Jane*?

23. In what item do the Five lower Timmy down into the catacombs from Smuggler's Top?

24. Is Yan, Charlie, Joe or Cuthbert the name of the young orphan boy the Five meet at Tremannon Farm?

25. Was Enid Blyton's second husband, Kenneth Waters, a children's book author, an air force pilot, a surgeon or a newspaper reporter?

26. In which month are the Famous Five reunited in *Five Fall Into Adventure*?

27. Do the Famous Five discover a diary, a gold bar or a diamond ring inside the box from the shipwreck in *Five On A Treasure Island*?

28. In *Five Go Off In A Caravan*, does Dick get help: from the circus, by flagging down a passing car or by phoning the police from the Mackies' farm?

29. Does Mr Durleston offer Mrs Philpot £100, £800, £2,000 or £4,000 for the door from Finniston Castle?

30. When Dick is kidnapped and held in Owl Dene, is he kept locked in the basement, the attic, the wood shed or the garage?

31. In *Five Fall Into Adventure*, is Jo's father an ex-acrobat, a newspaper reporter, a famous scientist or a spy?

32. Who does Anne run off to find after she sees Mr Curton fall in the quarry and hurt his leg: Uncle Quentin, Julian or Aunt Fanny?

33. Whilst tutoring the children, does Mr Roland stay in Kirrin Cottage, Kirrin Farm or the castle on Kirrin Island?

34. What item in Demon's Rocks lighthouse has the words 'Cast in 1896' on it: the giant lamp, a large brass bell or a wrought iron furnace?

35. Which member of the Famous Five spots the tall stone whilst on the raft on Gloomy Lake?

36. Who breaks his ankle whilst chasing the Five in *Five On A Hike Together*: Dirty Dick, Nailer, Luffy or Mr Gaston?

37. What, to their surprise, do the children find on their first visit to Mystery Moor: a train track, a deserted petrol station, a bus stop or an airstrip?

38. In *Five Have Plenty Of Fun*, how many days does Uncle Quentin say he has to go away for to meet Elbur Wright?

39. Whilst staying on Billycock Hill, do the Famous Five pay Toby, Mrs Thomas, Jeff or Mr Brent for food from Billycock Farm?

40. Which one of the following was not served at dinner by Joanna in *Five On A Secret Trail*: stuffed tomatoes, veal and ham pie, mashed potatoes, hard-boiled eggs?

41. In *Five Get Into A Fix*, who takes Mrs Thomas's note from Dick and Julian and tells them to forget all about it otherwise they will be sent home?

42. In *Five On A Secret Trail*, which of the Lawdler twins tells the Five his name first?

43. What colour is the trunk the Five find on the shipwreck by Kirrin Island?

44. Does Julian hire groundsheets and rugs for camping near Gloomy Lake from the Three Shepherds Inn, the post office or the farmers' market?

45. Can you name either of the two men who show visitors around the Wreckers' Cave at Demon's Rocks?

46. On their first trip to Mystery Moor, who goes with Dick, Julian and Anne instead of George?

47. How many brothers or sisters does Berta have?

48. What do the Famous Five find down the well in *Five Have A Mystery To Solve*: an iron door halfway down, a gold statue, a criminal hiding at the bottom or Wilfrid stuck on a ledge?

49. In *Five On A Hike Together*, which boat contains a waterproof sack full of stolen goods?

50. Which two children join the Famous Five in their hunt for treasure in the underground ruins of Finniston Castle?

QUIZ 9

1. At the start of the Famous Five series, who is the best swimmer in the group?

2. In *Five Run Away Together*, who do the Famous Five think tried to give Timothy poisoned meat?

3. How many towers did Faynights Castle originally have?

4. Does Timmy bite Mr Barling, the smuggler, on the leg, the bottom or the shoulder?

5. What is the name of the lake that the Famous Five camp close to in *Five Go Off In A Caravan*?

6. Does Timmy, George or Anne rescue Dick, Julian and Toby from Will Janes at the butterfly farm?

7. In *Five Get Into Trouble*, which of the Five accidentally eats some of Timmy's sausage meat sandwiches?

8. In *Five Go To Demon's Rocks*, by what name were One-Ear, Nosey and Bart known: the Three Wreckers, the Trio of Amigos, or the Three Smugglers?

9. In *Five Go Off To Camp*, who discovers the large lever that opens the bricked up railway tunnel?

10. According to Mrs Layman, her house overlooks the second biggest stretch of water in the world, but does she say the biggest is at San Francisco, Sydney or Shanghai?

11. What is the name of Bobby Loman's pet monkey: Chummy, Chippy, Charlie or Chester?

12. What is the first name, starting with the letter S, of the man who sleeps with a pantomime horse's head in *Five Go Down To The Sea*?

13. In *Five Fall Into Adventure*, Jo cannot: speak, swim or read and write?

14. When the Famous Five visit Kirrin Farm on Boxing Day, does Mrs Sanders give them plum pudding, chocolate cake or ginger buns?

15. Does George write, 'Simmy and Jake', 'Save Timmy', 'Red Tower' or 'Kirrin Island' inside the travellers' caravan when she is kidnapped?

16. Can you recall the first thing Sniffer says he wants when George says she will give him anything if he brings Timmy to her?

17. In *Five Have Plenty Of Fun*, who is the first to hear a motor-boat at night in the direction of Kirrin Island?

18. Which member of the Lenoir family is fond of playing practical jokes and exploring the catacombs?

19. What is the name of the first farm the Famous Five reach in their caravans in *Five Go Off In A Caravan*?

20. What item of his father's does Tinker find hidden in Charlie the chimpanzee's cage: his scientific papers, a travel clock or his portable radio?

21. Which member of the Famous Five is most suspicious of Martin, the boy they meet in *Five On Kirrin Island Again*?

22. Who keeps Olly's Farm at the end of *Five Go Off To Camp*, even though her husband is arrested by the police?

23. Is the name of Thurlow Kent's former bodyguard: Hunchy, Rooky, Ben or Perton?

24. Which adult does Timmy fling to the floor inside the Secret Way passage?

25. Which family do the Five spot on Kirrin Island in *Five Run Away Together*?

26. Are the two brainy boys that won scholarships at Julian and Dick's school called: Perkins and Cowell, Willis and Johnson or Baker and Andrews?

27. Do the Famous Five use a rowing boat, a small yacht, a raft or two canoes to explore Gloomy Lake?

28. In *Five Have A Wonderful Time*, what food does Timmy shy away from as it is one of the few he won't eat: salmon fillets, pickled onions, fruitcake or pork sausages?

29. Does George have to change trains at Great Giddings, Limming Ho or Middlecombe Woods to get to Faynights Castle?

30. On Mystery Moor, where do the Famous Five hide the parcels of money dropped from the aeroplane?

31. Was the first Famous Five book published in 1929, 1942, 1953 or 1966?

32. What is the name of Mrs Thomas's son, who she believed had been killed: Dai, Morgan, Llewellyn or Matthew?

33. Is Tiger Dan, Larry or Lou an acrobat in the circus?

34. Does Marybelle, Mrs Lenoir or Block serve the children their meals whilst they stay at Smuggler's Top?

35. Is the leader of the Barnies called Clopper, Red Tower or the Guv'nor?

36. What item of George's clothing does Timmy pull out of the caravan belonging to Gringo's mother?

37. In *Five On A Secret Trail*, is Sir John Lawdler the twins' uncle, father, brother or grandfather?

38. In *Five On A Secret Trail*, does Timmy cut his ear on pieces of glass, a thorny bush or some barbed wire?

39. When Will Janes is first arrested by the police, is it for stealing ducks, hitting children, kidnapping George or burgling houses?

40. Is Jo, Anita, Betty or Joanna the wife of Alfredo the fire-eater?

41. Who has massive eyebrows: the coastguard, Mr Curton, Tiger Dan or Mr Roland?

42. At the end of *Five Get Into A Fix*, whose birthday is celebrated with a roast turkey dinner: Julian's, Dick's or Morgan's?

43. In *Five On Finniston Farm*, what treasures do the Famous Five discover first: rows of daggers and swords, suits of armour, gold coins or gold jewellery?

44. Is the Famous Five and Tinker's first meal in the lighthouse: lunch, tea or tea-sup?

45. On their first full day at Demon's Rocks, the Famous Five and Tinker write postcards to Uncle Quentin and Aunt Fanny, Tinker's father and which one other person?

46. How many policemen enter the caves to arrest Tiger Dan and Lou?

47. Which member of the Famous Five steals a pork pie, cake and tin of biscuits from Maggie and Dirty Dick's tents?

48. Which famous author, who sent her a copy of his Winnie the Pooh book before it had gone on sale, did Enid Blyton interview in the 1920s?

49. Who steals the pages of Uncle Quentin's book containing the secret formula: Joanna, Mr Sanders, Mr Thomas the artist or Mr Roland?

50. Who had forgotten to lock the lighthouse and take the key with them when the lighthouse is burgled: Tinker, Dick, George or Anne?

QUIZ 10

1. Which dog with only one eye do the Famous Five encounter: Chummy, Jet, Bouncer or Barker?

2. Is Bufflo a whip-cracker, a snake-handler or a trapeze artist?

3. Can you recall either of the names, both beginning with the letter W, that the island in the middle of the harbour is called in *Five Have A Mystery To Solve*?

4. *Five On Finniston Farm* is set in which English county: Devon, Cornwall, Dorset or Somerset?

5. What time do the two Harries always get up at Finniston Farm: 6, 8 or 10 o'clock in the morning?

6. In *Five Get Into Trouble*, is 'sparklers' a name for: powerful flares used by smugglers, diamonds or policemen?

7. What is the name of the old housekeeper who lives at the butterfly farm in *Five Go To Billycock Hill*: Mrs James, Mrs Jones or Mrs Janes?

8. How do Tinker and the Famous Five travel from Kirrin to Demon's Rocks: by bicycle, in Aunt Fanny's car or by taxi?

9. In *Five On A Treasure Island*, which of the Five is kicked at the dinner table several times for nearly telling Aunt Fanny the children's secrets?

10. What team sport do the Five play near Two-Trees after discovering the boat at the bottom of Gloomy Lake?

11. In *Five Have Plenty Of Fun*, which member of the Famous Five is kidnapped when trying to put Sally into Timmy's kennel?

12. Who manages to unzip Julian and Dick from Clopper's costume in *Five Go Down To The Sea*?

13. How do the Famous Five get to Magga Glen farmhouse: by train, by bicycle, by car or by ferry boat?

14. In *Five Go Down To The Sea*, how many times does the shepherd say he has seen lights flash from the tower this year?

15. What colour is the two Harries' dog, Snippet?

16. In *Five On A Secret Trail*, under what sort of giant bush do the Famous Five make their camp after moving from the old ruined cottage?

17. According to his school report, viewed by Mr Roland, is Julian's weakest subject Latin, Geometry, French or Geography?

18. In *Five Are Together Again*, what is the name of the circus's band of musicians?

19. Which member of the Famous Five is the first to reach the top of Uncle Quentin's tower on Kirrin Island?

20. In *Five Go Down To The Sea*, which child annoys George by becoming very friendly with Timmy?

21. Is the elephant handler at the circus called Larry, Lou, Rossy or Lucilla?

22. In *Five Get Into A Fix*, who calls the hill that Old Towers stands on 'wicked': Mrs Jenkins, the shepherd, Aily or Morgan?

23. Did Uncle Quentin once spend a week in caves in Karlsbad, Cheddar or Mammoth Gorge?

24. In which book do the Famous Five meet the Lawdler twins: *Five Go Off To Camp*, *Five Get Into A Fix* or *Five On A Secret Trail*?

25. At what time in the morning does Uncle Quentin agree to signal Aunt Fanny from Kirrin Island: 8.00, 10.30 or 11.15?

26. Which of the following was not one of Enid Blyton's daughters: Imogen, Harriet, Gillian?

27. Was it Dobby, Perry or Sooty, a child at Dick and Julian's school, who always went on caravanning holidays?

28. When the Five frighten the Stick family in the castle dungeons, was George, Dick or Julian making cow noises?

29. Which of Mr and Mrs Lenoir's servants had been a spy and smuggler working with Mr Barling?

30. Wilfrid cannot go back home because his sister has which infectious disease?

31. In *Five Go To Mystery Moor*, do the Five find 30, 60, 90 or 120 parcels dropped by the aeroplane?

32. Is the airfield near Billycock Hill run by the Ministry of War, the Royal Air Force or a secret spy ring?

33. Who cuts the ropes that bind Dick, Julian and Jock inside the railway tunnel in *Five Go Off To Camp*?

34. Which fictional boarding school do twins Pat and Isobel O'Sullivan attend, along with Janet and Carlotta, in a six book series written by Enid Blyton?

35. In an Enid Blyton short story, which member of the Famous Five manages to find the missing famous racehorse lying in a cornfield?

36. Do the Famous Five show Mr Roland the piece of linen with the coded message on Christmas Eve, Christmas Day or Boxing Day?

37. What is the name of the small, nasty man who lives and works at Owl Dene: Roland, Hunchy, Wooden-Leg Sam or Jeremiah?

38. In *Five Go Off In A Caravan*, do the Famous Five buy a torch, a mirror, a notebook and pen or a quiz book as a present for Nobby?

39. As a child, Enid Blyton and two of her friends created a magazine called: *Dab*, *Three For Free* or *The Children's Gazette*?

40. Which of the Famous Five buys Timmy a new dog collar for Christmas in *Five Go Adventuring Again*?

41. Do the Five leave a railway timetable, a map of London or a postcard from their home to trick Mr and Mrs Stick into thinking they have returned home?

42. In *Five Have Plenty Of Fun*, when Anne goes to the shops to buy shoelaces, how many ice creams does she also purchase?

43. What was the name of the strolling players and entertainers who performed in farms and barns in *Five Go Down To The Sea*?

44. In *Five On A Treasure Island*, does Anne, Dick or Timmy fall down the well in the ruined castle?

45. What does Mr Barling use to navigate his way around the tunnels of Castaway Hill: chalk marks, a ball of string or a trail of breadcrumbs?

46. In which book does George first go to a boarding school?

47. How many flashes of the lantern is Uncle Quentin supposed to signal to Aunt Fanny from his tower on Kirrin Island at night: two, four or six?

48. In *Five Go Off To Camp*, do the Famous Five find a kidnapped girl, an old boat or boxes of valuable goods in the bricked-up railway tunnels?

49. Do Julian and Dick cycle at night to Fallenwick, Twining or Granton to rescue George?

50. What does Mrs Jones call the long sleigh Morgan uses to carry the Five's kit and food up the mountain at Magga Glen?

QUIZ 11

1. In *Five Fall Into Adventure*, which member of the Famous Five is drugged the night that Uncle Quentin's study is broken into?

2. What is the name of the hill on which Smuggler's Top is situated?

3. In *Five Go Off In A Caravan*, in which European country did Tiger Dan previously appear in circuses?

4. Do the Five dig down from a well, under the henhouse or down a rabbit hole to discover a tunnel that led to Finniston Castle's dungeons?

5. In the short story *Five Have A Puzzling Time*, Bobby Loman reached Kirrin Island on a blow-up bed: true or false?

6. Which member of the Famous Five is the first to see shimmering lights above Old Towers?

7. When Mischief throws raisins in the kitchen, who accidentally throws a cup of water all over Uncle Quentin?

8. Which boy goes down the tunnel with Dick and Julian to find George in *Five On Kirrin Island Again*?

9. In *Five Go Adventuring Again*, is the name of the children's tutor hired by Uncle Quentin over the Christmas holidays: Mr Thompson, Mr Kennedy, Miss Beech or Mr Roland?

10. In *Five Go To Mystery Moor*, is Ben the blacksmith about fifty, sixty-five or over eighty years old?

11. Which of the Famous Five gives Sniffer a red and white handkerchief to wipe his nose with, rather than rub it on his jacket sleeve?

12. Is the cat at Billycock Farm called Binky, Tinky, Curly or Cuddles?

13. What job is the boy called Sid doing when he is dragged into Kirrin Cottage by members of the Famous Five?

14. Can you name either of the two clowns listed on the circus posters in *Five Are Together Again*?

15. Who proves to be the fastest swimmer out of George, Dick or Berta?

16. Does Aunt Fanny, Julian, the coastguard or Joanna the cook sell lots of toys to Mr Curton?

17. With whom does Jeremiah Boogle have a small fight when he takes the Famous Five to Wreckers' Cave?

18. What is Mr Jenkins the gardener's first name: James, Ivor, Gregor or Rodney?

19. What is the name of the village that the Famous Five begin their hike from in *Five On A Hike Together*?

20. In which country is Richard Kent's father during most of the adventures in *Five Get Into Trouble*?

21. Who cuts Berta's hair really short to make her look like a boy: Julian, Anne or Aunt Fanny?

22. Which musical instrument did Enid Blyton specialise in when studying at the Guildhall School of Music?

23. How many tents do the Famous Five take on their camping trip in *Five Go Off To Camp*?

24. In *Five Have A Mystery To Solve*, what part of Timmy is grazed by a bullet: his paw, his ear or his tail?

25. In *Five On Kirrin Island Again*, is Uncle Quentin to signal from Kirrin Island once, twice or three times a day?

26. When Jo escapes the tower of Faynight Castle, does she go to Uncle Quentin, the police or Uncle Alfredo for help?

27. What two weapons does Julian take from the underground ruins of Finniston Castle dungeons before the Famous Five flee?

28. In *Five Are Together Again*, which member of Tappin's Circus does George discover on Kirrin Island?

29. Can you name any one of the three named adults in *Five On A Secret Trail* involved with the crime of stealing and hiding the top secret blueprints?

30. In which building do the Famous Five enter the passage known as the Secret Way?

31. In the Adventure series, is the name of the children's pet parrot Squawker, Ralph, Kiki or Basil?

32. Is the coastguard making his grandson a toy car, aeroplane or windmill when the Famous Five meet him in *Five On Kirrin Island Again*?

33. After George sees a face at the window of Kirrin Cottage, who is sent to stay in the room where Joanna and Berta are sleeping?

34. Who calls off the three farm dogs that attack Timmy in *Five Get Into A Fix*?

35. Is *Robin Hood*, *Beauty and the Beast* or *101 Dalmatians* showing at the cinema in the short story *Five And A Half-Term Adventure*?

36. In *Five On A Treasure Island*, what does the map from the shipwreck show: Kirrin Cottage, Polseath Town Hall or the ruined castle on Kirrin Island?

37. Who rigs up a buzzer which sounds when people enter the children's wing of Smuggler's Top?

38. In *Five Go Off To Camp*, is Mr Luffy, Anne or Dick outside the railway tunnel when the other members of the Famous Five are caught inside?

39. In *Five Go Adventuring Again*, does Anne call the new doll she gets for Christmas: Wendy-Woo, Betsy-May or Kerri-Ann?

40. Do the fair folk plan to rescue the Famous Five from Faynights Castle using a peg rope, a wooden ladder or some life jackets?

41. What covers up the passageway to the caves found underneath the caravans: a steel plate, planks and heather or large tree trunks?

42. Which of the Famous Five is the first to see a scientist in the tower of Faynights Castle through field glasses?

43. In *Five Run Away Together*, does George call visitors to her island vagrants, trippers, hitch-hikers or interlopers?

44. Is Edgar Stick older or younger than Anne?

45. Are the stolen goods recovered from the boat in Gloomy Lake rare paintings, jewellery or bundles of passports and notebooks?

46. Does Anne, Dick or Julian tell Nobby all about the fabulous adventures the Famous Five have been on in the past?

47. What is Mr Sanders the farmer's first name: Rusty, John, Peter or Michael?

48. In *Five On A Treasure Island*, what does Julian turn upside-down and pretend is a shipwreck, annoying George's father as a result?

49. Who places the fake notebook under the stone in the garden of Kirrin Cottage in *Five Fall Into Adventure*?

50. Which character in *Five Go To Billycock Hill* has no teeth and hates insects: Will Janes, Mr Brent, Mr Gringle or Mrs Janes?

QUIZ 12

1. Was Enid Blyton's first published book called *The Six Cousins*, *The Wishing Chair* or *Child Whispers*?

2. What expensive food item does Richard Kent buy to share with the Famous Five: a whole smoked ham, a chocolate cake or a fillet of salmon?

3. Which pantomime have Dick, Julian and Anne been hoping to see in *Five Go Adventuring Again*?

4. What sport does the elephant at the circus have enormous fun playing with the Famous Five?

5. In *Five Go Off To Camp*, what card game do the Famous Five play with Mr Luffy: poker, rummy, blackjack or happy families?

6. In which Famous Five book do the children discover gold ingots in Kirrin Castle?

7. What does Bufflo remove from Jeffrey Pottersham's hand using his whip?

8. Does Anne, Julian or George discover the entrance to the dungeons of Kirrin Castle?

9. Which part of his body does Guy Lawdler injure underground: his back, his elbow, his knee or his ankle?

10. Which of the Five is the first to climb down the rope into the well in *Five Have A Mystery To Solve*?

11. In which book are the children entertained in a barn in Cornwall by acts including singers, dancers and two men in a horse costume?

12. How many children do Mr and Mrs Sanders from Kirrin Farm have: none, one, two or three?

13. Which of the two Harries at Finniston Farm could be identified by a small scar on their hand?

14. Is Dai, Gwyneth, Fany or Billy the name of the little lamb that follows Aily everywhere?

15. How many children does Mrs Penruthlan, at Tremannon Farm, have?

16. In *Five On A Secret Trail*, which member of the Famous Five removes the rope that the three criminals have used to travel underground?

17. For how many weeks is Berta to stay at Kirrin Cottage?

18. Does Anne, Guy Lawdler, Dick or Harry Lawdler faint whilst underground?

19. Does the aeroplane flying over Mystery Moor drop a load of cargo on its first, second or third flight?

20. Which scientist captures Jo and locks the other children in the castle tower in *Five Have A Wonderful Time*?

21. What is the name of the hill on which Owl Dene house sits?

22. In *Five Have A Mystery To Solve*, was Sally, Sarah, Susie or Samantha the name of the woman who helped cook and clean at Mrs Layman's cottage?

23. What colour shirt is Aily wearing when she first meets some of the Famous Five on the mountain?

24. In *Five Have Plenty Of Fun*, what type of dog is Sally: a black poodle, a Scottish terrier or a brown spaniel?

25. What rank does Toby's cousin have in the air force: captain, flight-lieutenant, squadron leader or corporal?

26. Which of the Famous Five nicknames Tinker the dog, Stinker?

27. Which two of the Famous Five get into the pantomime horse costume at Tremannon Farm?

28. How much does Dick pay for his and Anne's accommodation for a night at Mrs Taggart's house: 25p, £1.00, £2.00 or £5.00?

29. Which member of the Famous Five has an interest in antiques and second-hand shops?

30. In *Five Fall Into Adventure*, who offers to let Jo stay with her after her father is arrested?

31. Which character from *Five Fall Into Adventure* do the Famous Five meet again in *Five Have A Wonderful Time*?

32. On the first night of their hike in *Five On A Hike Together*, do Julian and George end up sleeping at Spiggy House, the Three Shepherds Inn or Blue Pond Farm?

33. In *Five Go To Mystery Moor*, George arranges for Timmy to take a note to: Julian, Sniffer, Henrietta or Dick?

34. Who manages to open the mechanical gates to let the police into Owl Dene: George, Dick, Julian or Anne?

35. Who tells the Famous Five about the history of Finniston Castle: Trevor Philpot, William Finniston or Mr Henning?

36. On the first day camping in *Five Go Off To Camp*, does Mr Luffy leave his tent to hunt for deer, a butterfly or a rare bird?

37. What colour is the paint Timmy knocks over and spills when the Famous Five visit the coastguard's cottage?

38. Who put up Uncle Quentin's tower on Kirrin Island: Oxford University, an oil company or the Ministry of Research?

39. What vehicle do the two criminals in the short story *A Lazy Afternoon* use to try and make their escape?

40. At the start of *Five Are Together Again*, which of the Five insists on getting a taxi to Kirrin Cottage rather than walking from the station?

41. Do the Famous Five park their caravans at the Mackies' Farm, on Merren Hills, or beside the shore of Merren Lake?

42. At Smuggler's Top, whose nose turns white at the tip when they are angry?

43. Is Elbur Wright an American scientist, the ringmaster of a travelling circus or a newspaper journalist?

44. Is *The Traveller, The Roamer* or *The Voyager* the name of the ship used by the kidnappers in *Five Run Away Together*?

45. How much does the man pretending to be Mr Brent give Dick and Julian for the butterfly they capture: fifty pence, £5.00 or £25.00?

46. What is the name of the butler at Smuggler's Top: Block, Sanders, Jenkins or Campbell?

47. John Polpenny is: the owner of Tremannon Farm, the innkeeper at Polwilly Halt or the railway porter at Kirrin Station?

48. In *Five Go Adventuring Again*, have the two boys or the two girls in the Famous Five been ill twice with flu in the same term?

49. In *Five Go Off In A Caravan*, which horse tries to throw Nobby off: Trotter, Black Queen or Fury?

50. Who orders Markhoff to shoot Timmy the dog dead?

QUIZ 13

1. Whose bike gets a puncture in *Five Get Into Trouble*?

2. Is Sir John Lawdler a famous historian, scientist or explorer?

3. Where does Tinker tell the Famous Five he wants to hide all his father's important scientific papers: on Kirrin Island, in the circus caravans or in Demon's Cave?

4. Is Dr Drew, Dr Johnson or Dr Figgis the doctor who treats the Five in *Five Get Into A Fix*?

5. Was Finniston Castle built by the ancient Romans, the Normans or the Tudors?

6. Which one of the following is not one of Morgan's seven dogs: Doon, Rafe, Bryn or Hal?

7. Which fifteen book series written by Enid Blyton features Fatty, Pip, Bets, Larry and Daisy solving mysteries in the village of Peterswood?

8. Who owns the sweetshop at Demon's Rocks: Jack, Tom, Jeremiah or Jacob?

9. In *Five Have Plenty Of Fun*, Anne rescues the rest of the Famous Five by calling the police: true or false?

10. When Markhoff, Carl and Tom search for the Famous Five, does Markhoff tread on Jo, Julian or Dick's hand?

11. In which book does Mr Barling try to stop marshes being drained by kidnapping Uncle Quentin?

12. Which millionaire's daughter is kidnapped in *Five Run Away Together*: Harry Armstrong, Cornelius Wyatt or Frederick Thompson?

13. In *Five Have A Mystery To Solve*, does Lucas work in the town park, at the swimming pool or on the golf course?

14. When Wilfrid rows to Whispering Island and meets the Famous Five is he carrying a mouse, a baby hedgehog or an adder snake in his pocket?

15. At the start of *Five Go To Demon's Rocks*, which professor friend of Uncle Quentin's visits Kirrin Cottage?

16. What item does Dick bet George that she won't take breakfast up to Junior Henning at Finniston Farm?

17. What crime occurs in the short story *George's Hair Is Too Long*: a robbery, a kidnapping or the theft of some racehorses?

18. Which lost child do the Famous Five go searching for in *Five Go To Billycock Hill*: Toby, Sooty or Benny?

19. What is the first butterfly the Five see Mr Gringle catch: a Blue Captain, a Red Admiral or a Brown Argus?

20. In *Five Have Plenty Of Fun*, do Dick, Julian and Timmy enter the house which holds George through the back door, the coal hole or through an underground passage from the garden?

21. What object of Julian's is stolen in the lighthouse burglary: his watch, his radio, his field glasses or his travelling clock?

22. Is George taken in a caravan, a canal boat or the boot of a car by Gringo from the fairground to the house in Twining?

23. Despite having no electricity at their farmhouse, which device do Mr and Mrs Penruthlan sometimes enjoy?

24. Can you name one of the three men that fight inside Red's house allowing Jo to escape and join up with the Famous Five?

25. In *Five Go Off To Camp*, what sort of fruit tree grows beside Jock's bedroom, allowing him to climb from the ground up into the room?

26. Is George, Dick or Anne the first to get into the bricked up tunnel and see a spook train in *Five Go Off To Camp*?

27. Does Richard, Julian or Dick hide in the boot of Mr Perton's car in order to escape and alert the police?

28. Does Timmy, George or Dick carry Uncle Quentin's important notebook back from Kirrin Island to Kirrin Cottage?

29. On visiting the circus, who is the first of the Five to shake hands with the chimpanzee?

30. Which member of the staff at Smuggler's Top do the Famous Five play a trick on whilst they hide behind the curtains?

31. What tool do Julian and George use to break down the dungeon door of Kirrin Castle?

32. Do Ebenezer and Jacob chase Dick and Julian, Anne and George or Tinker and Mischief through the tunnels near the Wreckers' Cave?

33. Which of the following is not one of Jennifer Armstrong's dolls: Rosebud, Lily, Marigold or Josephine?

34. What is Timmy the dog chasing when he falls down the well in the ruined castle on Kirrin Island?

35. Which member of the Famous Five is cut on the cheek by splinters from the dungeon door of Kirrin Castle?

36. Had Nobby's, Sooty's or Jennifer's father been a clown in a circus?

37. What is the name of Aggie's brother in *Five Get Into Trouble*?

38. At the start of *Five Go To Mystery Moor*, who declares they have been bored all week?

39. In the short story *Five And A Half-Term Adventure*, what has been stolen by a man and woman and wrapped in a shawl to pretend it was a baby?

40. In *Five Go Adventuring Again*, is Mr Wilton an artist, a smuggler, a farmer or a policeman?

41. Does Trotter, Fury or Dobby pull the green caravan in *Five Go Off In A Caravan*?

42. The Wreckers' Way starts at the cove by the sea but ends in a shed on which farm?

43. Which of the Five receives the fairy from the top of the Christmas tree from Mr Roland?

44. In *Five On Kirrin Island Again*, is Martin a talented musician, mountain climber or artist?

45. Which member of the fair staying in Faynights Field turns out to be Jo's uncle?

46. Whose handkerchief does Nobby steal from the caravan: Anne's, George's, Dick's or Uncle Quentin's?

47. In *Five On A Hike Together*, what does Julian say the ringing bells signal?

48. Enid Blyton's nephew, Carey Blyton, devised which characters that featured in books, TV programmes and in their own stage shows for young children?

49. In *Five Go Adventuring Again*, is Uncle Quentin working on a cure to a disease, a new type of engine or a secret formula?

50. Is the money that the Famous Five find in *Five Go To Mystery Moor* in British pounds or American dollars?

QUIZ 14

1. What is the name of the man paid to kidnap Berta in *Five Have Plenty Of Fun*?

2. As a young woman, what did Enid Blyton train to become: a nurse, a teacher or a plumber?

3. What colour signal does Nobby wave from the boat to warn the Famous Five not to visit the circus?

4. In *Five Get Into A Fix*, what does Anne say the Welsh word 'bach' means in English: strong, danger, little or help?

5. To which lady does Julian donate the money given to the Famous Five by Mr Perton?

6. Which of the Famous Five rides with Henrietta on one horse as they escape the travellers?

7. In which book does Aunt Fanny have an operation and Timmy have a fight with another dog, called Tinker?

8. What does Timmy receive as a reward for his part in foiling the dog thieves in the short story *Five And A Half-Term Adventure*?

9. Which compass direction does the kitchen in Kirrin Farm face?

10. At the start of the Famous Five series, who is the weakest swimmer out of Anne, Dick and Julian?

11. Does George speak to a reporter from the *Daily Sketch*, *The Saturday News* or the *Daily Clarion* at the start of *Five Fall Into Adventure*?

12. Which one of the following did Enid Blyton not write: *The Naughtiest Girl* series, the *Mistletoe Farm* series or *The Secret Garden*?

13. What is the name of Berta's dog?

14. Who is the boss of the travellers, beginning with the letter B, who had ordered them to head to Mystery Moor?

15. Does the Secret Way lead to the castle on Kirrin Island, the old inn in Polseath or Kirrin Farmhouse?

16. Who tells the Famous Five at Smuggler's Top that he will have a dog poisoned if it is caught?

17. Who do the Five imprison in the Kirrin Castle dungeons in *Five Run Away Together*?

18. Which two members of the Famous Five, along with Sooty, investigate the light from the tower of Smuggler's Top?

19. In *Five Go To Billycock Hill*, which relative of Toby's is accused of stealing a top secret aircraft?

20. Which two of the following men threaten the Famous Five in their caravans: Mr Mackie, Tiger Dan, Mr Roland, Block, Lou?

21. Does Aggie hide a meal for the Famous Five in the flower beds, the old woodshed or the henhouse?

22. In *Five Are Together Again*, can Mr Tapper, Jeremy, Madelon or Mr Wooh answer complicated maths questions in a fraction of a second?

23. Which character in *Five On Kirrin Island Again* lost his mother at a young age and says he didn't go to school because he had been ill?

24. In *Five Fall Into Adventure*, what does Dick buy Jo after losing their contest on the beach?

25. In *Five On A Hike Together*, what hill is the first of the four short messages on the piece of paper handed to Dick by the escaped prisoner?

26. In *Five Have A Wonderful Time*, which of the Five do Jeffrey Pottersham and three other men plan to take as a hostage?

27. Who does Mrs Penruthlan threaten to beat after he has told her that her husband may be a smuggler?

28. What animal has a message written on him by the two trapped pilots in *Five Go To Billycock Hill*?

29. What colour are the wings of the American car used to kidnap George in *Five Have Plenty Of Fun*?

30. What one word, beginning with the letter G, is written on the note George leaves for the others when she is kidnapped in *Five Have Plenty Of Fun*?

31. Does Cecil Dearlove insist on playing soldiers, going birdwatching, doing maths lessons or shoplifting in town when he visits Jock?

32. What object do the Famous Five and Harry Lawdler find underground that contains important blueprints?

33. What reward does Jeff promise the Famous Five for saving him and Ray: new bicycles, a flight in a plane or money?

34. Which member of the Famous Five starts crying and doesn't want to stay any longer at Magga Glen after Timmy is attacked in *Five Get Into A Fix*?

35. Who does Mr Henning bring to Finniston to advise him about buying lots of old things from the farm?

36. When having supper with the fair folk in Faynights Field, does George, Jo or Anne scream when she sees a snake?

37. What fruit does Julian bring with him whilst he hides on top of the caravan to spy on Lou and Tiger Dan?

38. Which of the Famous Five watches Mr Roland hand over Uncle Quentin's papers to the two artists?

39. In *Five Go Down To The Sea*, is Yan's great-grandfather a shepherd, farmer, fisherman or coastguard?

40. What sort of creature is Nosey: a donkey, a tame fox, a jackdaw bird or a small dog?

41. Wilfrid returns to the golf course to search for what item he has lost: a baby hedgehog, his pocket knife, his whistle or his map of the lighthouse?

42. In *Five Have A Mystery To Solve*, the boy hiring boats says they cost £3.00 an hour, but how much for a week?

43. In which book do the Famous Five recover the diamond necklace stolen from the Queen of Fallonia?

44. In *Five Are Together Again*, how many doors does Professor Hayling have to unlock in order to reach the room at the top of his tower at Big Hollow?

45. Is the light on top of Demon's Rocks lighthouse powered by electricity, gas or paraffin oil?

46. Is the book that Anne and George see the boy reading in *Five On A Secret Trail* about pirates and smugglers, battles and warfare, archaeology or spying?

47. In *Five On A Treasure Island*, what does Aunt Fanny serve the children for their first breakfast on holiday: cold porridge, smoked kippers or bacon and eggs?

48. Is Jock, Cecil or Martin the name of the boy who lives at Olly's Farm?

49. Was an underground metal mine, a kidnapped family or a large collection of stolen paintings and jewels found in the hill beneath Old Towers house?

50. Which place does Anne declare to be the most exciting she has ever stayed in: Finniston Farm, Kirrin Island or Demon's Rocks lighthouse?

QUIZ 15

1. Had Jo's mother worked in the circus as: a tightrope walker, a clown, a dog trainer or a lion tamer?

2. How many bunk beds are there in the hut on the mountainside in *Five Get Into A Fix*?

3. Which one of the following is not a boat available to hire in *Five Have A Mystery To Solve*: *Splasho*, *Seagull* or *Saucy Sue*?

4. Is the chapel of Finniston Castle used as a henhouse, a grain store or a milking shed?

5. Which member of the Famous Five most disliked Mr Roland the tutor as soon as they met?

6. What sort of bird builds its nest in the towers of the ruined castle on Kirrin Island?

7. From which city do newspaper men travel to Kirrin Cottage to interview Uncle Quentin about the shipwreck?

8. Can you name any two of the four men that climb Faynights Castle to rescue the Famous Five?

9. In *Five Go Adventuring Again*, which two members of the Famous Five do not visit Kirrin Farm on Boxing Day?

10. Apart from a raft, how many boats do the Five discover in the old boathouse on Gloomy Lake?

11. In 1960, were two, six or eleven new Noddy books published?

12. Does Rooky, Hunchy, Aggie or Thurlow Kent throw a shoebrush at Julian's head?

13. From which city do Uncle Quentin and Aunt Fanny send a telegram in *Five Fall Into Adventure*: Seville, Paris, Rome or Hamburg?

14. Does a storm, intruders or someone stealing their tent force George and Anne to stay in the old, ruined cottage in *Five On A Secret Trail*?

15. Is Mr Andrews: Jock's father, his stepfather, his uncle or a family friend?

16. Is the man who rents the cottage next to the coastguard's cottage called Mr Roland, Mr Clarkson, Mr Reynolds or Mr Curton?

17. In *Five Have Plenty Of Fun*, does Jim work in a hotel, a garage, a hospital or at the fairground?

18. On the Five's first trip to Kirrin Island, who rows the boat the whole way over: George, Dick or Julian?

19. In *Five Get Into A Fix* does the underground tunnel to Old Towers end up in wine cellars, the kitchen larder or the henhouse?

20. Can you name either of the men who enter the treasure room on Whispering Island and lock the Famous Five inside?

21. What is the name of Pierre Lenoir's sister?

22. What does Dick steal from under the arm of Sid, of the Barnies, which contains the smuggled goods?

23. From which country has the aeroplane which dropped parcels in *Five Go To Mystery Moor* flown?

24. When the Famous Five help Toby with his chores at Billycock Farm, which pair weed the flower garden?

25. What does Aily's father do for a living? Is he a vegetable farmer, a miner, a shepherd or a policeman?

26. Does it snow before, during or after Christmas Day in *Five Go Adventuring Again*?

27. Which of the Lawdler twins do the Famous Five find howling and crying at the Roman camp?

28. When the Famous Five head off on their first ever caravan holiday, what colour is the caravan that Anne chooses to live in?

29. Is the kidnap ransom for Jennifer Armstrong: £100,000, £1 million or £10 million?

30. Does George, Mrs Mackie, Lucilla or Rossy nurse Barker back to health?

31. In *Five Go Off In A Caravan*, had Tiger Dan and Lou's robberies been worrying the police for six months, over a year or four years?

32. What does the Latin phrase *via occulta* mean in English: 'keep out', 'secret way' or 'hidden treasure'?

33. What is the name of the farm that the Famous Five plan to sleep at on the first night of their walk in *Five On A Hike Together*?

34. In the short story *When Timmy Chased The Cat*, what is the name of the big black cat the Famous Five spot at Tarley's Mount?

35. How many people live at the butterfly farm near Billycock Hill: one, two, three or four?

36. Are Darrell Rivers and Gwendoline Mary Lacey characters in Blyton's Five Find-Outers, The Secret Seven or Malory Towers series?

37. Did Jock live on Owl Farm, Lowton's Farm or Burrow Farm before moving to Olly's Farm?

38. What is the last hot meal the Famous Five have before heading off to the mountain hut in *Five Get Into A Fix*: steak and kidney pie, a roast beef dinner or eggs, bacon and sausages?

39. What is the name of the place where the Lenoir family live: Blue Pond Farmhouse, Demon's Cove or Smuggler's Top?

40. What item thrown through a tower window in Faynights Castle alarms the Famous Five?

41. What are the names of the two men with Mr Perton and Rooky: John and Jack, Pete and Edward or Ben and Fred?

42. How many policemen accompany the Five when they go and find the hidden money on Mystery Moor?

43. Whose bike does Jo borrow at night to ride to Granton to question a member of the travelling fair about George's disappearance?

44. In *Five On A Secret Trail*, is the boy digging to find ancient Roman, Iron Age or Anglo-Saxon objects?

45. In *Five Are Together Again*, did Oliver Cromwell, Henry VIII or Queen Victoria give the field next to Big Hollow to the Hayling family?

46. According to the shopkeeper, is the Demon's Rocks lighthouse over 60, 90 or 120 years old?

47. Mr Penruthlan says he is going to give the Clopper costume away to friends of his. Who do those friends turn out to be?

48. Which person at Billycock Farm previously had a lamb and two baby geese as pets?

49. After they explore the shaft under the lighthouse, who surprises the Famous Five by appearing in the lighthouse: Police Constable Sharp, Jeremiah Boogle or Uncle Quentin?

50. In *Five Go Adventuring Again*, which adult can't bear to see Timothy suffering in the snow and brings him inside Kirrin Cottage?

QUIZ 16

1. When Uncle Quentin reaches the marshes surrounding Smuggler's Top, is he dressed in a business suit, running shorts and vest or his pyjamas?

2. In *Five Go Off In A Caravan*, what drink – a favourite of the Famous Five – can be found in the locker underneath the second caravan?

3. Is the name of Richard Kent's holiday tutor Roland, Lomax, Jenkins or Luffy?

4. Does Berta, Gringo or Spiky call Timmy a mongrel, upsetting George as a result?

5. Does James, Alf or Martin help prepare George's boat so that she can travel to Kirrin Island on her own in *Five On Kirrin Island Again*?

6. In which room of Finniston Farmhouse is there a solid oak door leading from the old Finniston Castle?

7. In *Five Get Into A Fix*, which two of the Five go for a walk in the mountains on their first full day in Wales?

8. Does Anita, Anne, George or Bufflo chase Alfredo with a saucepan after he has burnt food in their caravan?

9. In *Five On A Treasure Island*, what weapon does the man threaten to kill Timmy with?

10. Which one of the following is not a game the Five take on their first caravan holiday: Ludo, Happy Families or Monopoly?

11. Which man with shaggy eyebrows, a yachting cap and a long pipe do the Famous Five and Tinker encounter on the quayside at Demon's Rocks?

12. What creature terrifies Jeffrey Pottersham and the three other men so much that they stop trying to escape from Faynights Castle and hide in the room in the tower?

13. Who brings handy tools to help the Five remove the stone slab by the water spring in *Five On A Secret Trail*?

14. Which of the Five finds the pump that gives them fresh water when they stay at the ruins of Two-Trees?

15. In what short story does Bobby Loman come to Kirrin Island for a holiday?

16. What complete word, beginning with the letter C, is printed on Curly the pig's body in *Five Go To Billycock Hill*?

17. The Five are shocked to discover that how many aircraft have been stolen from Billycock Hill airfield: one, two or three?

18. Which child tells Mr Wooh all about Professor Hayling's inventions, including the sko-wheel?

19. Which member of the Famous Five leads Sooty Lenoir and Uncle Quentin out of the tunnels of Castaway Hill?

20. What do the children find inside what they thought was the smuggler's trunk in *Five Run Away Together*?

21. On their first ever visit to Kirrin Island, do the Famous Five eat ham sandwiches, Cornish pasties or fresh fish?

22. Which one of the following wears the head and front legs of Clopper the pantomime horse: Mr Penruthlan, Mr Binks, Mr Roth or Mr Roland?

23. In *Five Fall Into Adventure,* when Dick rides Sid's bike, where does he go and sit inside for a while before returning to Kirrin Cottage at night?

24. In *Five On A Secret Trail*, does Harry, Dick, George or Anne find the white arrow chalked on the cave wall to guide them in the right direction?

25. What is Mr Henning's final offer for the treasure on Finniston Farm: £10,000, £50,000 or £100,000?

26. Who leads Julian, Dick and Anne out of Ravens Wood when they get lost?

27. Does Timmy, Julian or Anne discover the sliding panel beside the grandfather clock at Kirrin Farm?

28. When the Five leave Captain Johnson's Riding School, do they camp high on the moors, down in the quarry or beside a lake?

29. What part of Dick's body is injured and bruised after Mr Penruthlan grabs him during the stormy night?

30. Is Killy's Yard, the Merran Hills or Crowleg Vale the site of some of Britain's rarest beetles, according to Mr Luffy?

31. Does the police inspector who arrests Lou and Tiger Dan eat chocolate, bread and honey or bacon and eggs with the Famous Five?

32. Which of the Five brought new field glasses (binoculars) to Faynights Field in *Five Have A Wonderful Time*?

33. What happens to the boat the Five use to get to Whispering Island? Is it: smashed up by criminals, washed away by a strong tide or stolen by Wilfrid?

34. Is George's favourite walk from Kirrin Cottage by the lake, over the cliffs or through the woods?

35. In *Five Go Adventuring Again*, the secret message on the linen mentions a room with how many wooden panels?

36. At whose house were the items stolen from Demon's Rocks lighthouse found: Jeremiah Boogle's, Jacob Loomer's or Professor Hayling's?

37. In *Five On A Hike Together*, there are four short messages on the piece of paper handed to Dick by the escaped prisoner. Is the third message 'Chimney', 'Maggie' or 'Saucy Jane'?

38. Which member of the Famous Five chops up the three men's motor-boat so they cannot escape Kirrin Island?

39. In *Five Go Adventuring Again*, which adult does Timmy bite first?

40. Does the passage under the sea from Kirrin Island come out inside Kirrin Cottage, the old quarry or the coastguard's cottage?

41. Do the Famous Five find the kidnapped girl called Jennifer in the castle dungeons, in the shipwreck or in a clearing in the wood?

42. How much does Mr Durleston offer the Philpot family for the rights to dig up the kitchen-midden on Finniston Farm: £5,000, £10,000, £25,000 or £50,000?

43. Who makes the Famous Five some unpleasant sandwiches with stale bread at the start of *Five Run Away Together*?

44. Does Timmy, Julian or Aunt Fanny carry a note to Dick and Anne signed 'Georgina' in *Five On A Treasure Island*?

45. As a baby, Enid Blyton nearly died of which disease: scarlet fever, malaria, tuberculosis or whooping cough?

46. In the short story *Happy Christmas, Five!*, who follows the Christmas present thief from Kirrin Cottage into Kirrin Village?

47. What colour is the broken comb owned by George that the rest of the Famous Five discover when they search for her?

48. In *Five Have A Mystery To Solve*, what is in the second box filled with sawdust that the Five open: a statue of an angel, a gold dagger, a silver crown or an old book?

49. Which circus man beats Nobby for making friends with the Famous Five: Rossy, Lou or Tiger Dan?

50. Does the land where the Famous Five plan to camp in *Five Get Into Trouble* belong to Thurlow Kent, Aunt Fanny and Uncle Quentin or Mr Perton?

QUIZ 17

1. Enid Blyton's twelve-year-old daughter named the horses that featured in *Six Cousins At Mistletoe Farm*: true or false?

2. Which member of the Lenoir family really doesn't like dogs but shakes Timmy's paw?

3.   Who has developed plans to drain the marshes that surround Smuggler's Top: Mr Barling, Uncle Quentin or Mr Sanders?

4.   Is Richard Kent twelve and blond-haired, thirteen and brown-haired or fourteen and dark-haired?

5.   After rescuing George from Gringo in *Five Have Plenty Of Fun*, what is the first meal the Famous Five eat: breakfast, lunch, high tea or supper?

6.   How many years old does Nobby say he is?

7.   Can you name any two of the members of the Secret Seven, a series of books written by Enid Blyton?

8.   In *Five Go Adventuring Again*, does Anne, Dick or George accidentally spill a water jug in the artist's bedroom, alerting the adults outside the door?

9.   What sort of shop does Mr Pails run: a greengrocers, a sweetshop, a camping shop or an ironmongers?

10. In *Five Are Together Again*, who thinks he is taking Professor Hayling's papers to Kirrin Island but was tricked by George?

11. In *Five Run Away Together*, is Mr Roland, Edgar, Alf or Mr Sanders to let the Famous Five know when George's parents return home from hospital?

12. Does Richard first meet the Five at Croker's Corner, Middlecombe Woods or the Green Pool?

13. Do the police, the fishermen or men from the Ministry of Research come and rescue Uncle Quentin, Martin and the Five from the tunnels under the sea?

14. In *Five On A Treasure Island*, which of the Five retrieves the map after it has blown from Julian's hands into the water?

15. Can you name any one of the three dogs that attack and bite Timmy on the Five's first full day at Magga Glen farm?

16. In *Five Fall Into Adventure*, does Jo, Jake or Markhoff bring the ransom note for George and Timmy?

17. Who does Julian have to send a card to every day whilst on holiday in *Five Go Off In A Caravan*?

18. Which member of the Famous Five rescues Uncle Quentin and Sooty by chasing away Mr Barling and Block?

19. Which two children are led by Timmy over Mystery Moor to find George and Anne, who are being held prisoner?

20. Under which name did Enid Blyton sometimes write: Hilda Garforth, Mary Pollock or Davis Marshall?

21. In *Five On A Hike Together*, does Julian reckon one of the necklaces they find is worth £100, £10,000, £100,000 or £1,000,000?

22. Which fisher boy at Kirrin Island did George get to look after Timmy the dog?

23. The men who kidnap Oliver in *Good Old Timmy!* lock him up: in the boot of their car, in a shed in a field, in a large wooden box or in Julian and Dick's caravan?

24. What two colours are the strange lights that shine when the Famous Five camp in the ruined cottage in *Five On A Secret Trail*?

25. Do the Five get the bus to Tinkers Green to visit Faynights Castle, to see the sea and talk to fishermen or to go to the circus?

26. Which of the Famous Five has some hairs removed by the whip-cracker in *Five Have A Wonderful Time*?

27. Who has an Auntie Gwen who agrees to let the Famous Five stay at her house: Mr Jenkins, Dr Drew or Uncle Quentin?

28. What is the first thing the Famous Five discover in the hidey-hole at Kirrin Farm: a book of recipes, a tobacco pouch or a secret map?

29. Can you name two of the five dogs, all starting with the letter B, that Richard Kent tells the Famous Five he owns?

30. Is the surname of the kidnapped girl in *Five Run Away Together*: Jackson, Armstrong, Halpern or Clark?

31. Does Julian buy three, six or nine big loaves from the bakers before the Famous Five flee to Kirrin Island in *Five Run Away Together*?

32. What item of Uncle Quentin's do the men who kidnap George and Timmy want in return for them?

33. What nickname, beginning with the letter K, do many local people use for the strange island in the harbour in *Five Have A Mystery To Solve*?

34. Which character in *Five Go To Billycock Hill* had fallen in with bad men and given his mother a black eye?

35. Does Julian pay Jo, Spiky, Jim or Berta a pound for ringing round local villages to try and find where the big American car has gone?

36. In *Five On A Treasure Island*, does George say the shipwreck carried silver jewellery, gold bars or diamonds and rubies?

37. Which member of the Famous Five is hit in the head by a cinder thrown by a man in *Five Go Off To Camp*?

38. Which man and woman get trapped in the Green Marshes as they chase after the Famous Five in *Five On A Hike Together*?

39. Who is camping only a quarter of a mile away from the Five's tents on Mystery Moor: Captain Johnson, Henrietta or the travellers?

40. Who do the Five think was a smuggler in Cornwall, but turns out to be working with the police to try and catch smugglers?

41. Which two of the following men catch and tie up most of the Five in railway tunnels in *Five Go Off To Camp*: Mr Luffy, Mr Andrews, Cecil Dearlove, Mr Peters?

42. In *Five Go Off In A Caravan*, in the caravans the Famous Five travel in, is the water tank on the roof, inside the cabin or slung underneath the wheels?

43. What is the name of the secret route along the coast used by smugglers and shipwreck hunters in *Five Go Down To The Sea*?

44. At the end of *Five Go Adventuring Again*, do the police arrive at Kirrin Cottage by car, motorcycles, on skis or in a motorboat?

45. Who snoops on the Famous Five when they are discussing Finniston Castle: Harriet Philpot, Mr Durleston or Junior Henning?

46. Which boy do Dick and Julian meet under the giant oak tree near the butterfly farm in *Five Go To Billycock Hill*?

47. Does George, Uncle Quentin, Mr Curton or Julian smash up the glass room at the top of the tower on Kirrin Island?

48. Which item do the Five not see in the shipwreck in *Five On A Treasure Island*: cabin bunk beds, a brass cannon or the cook's pots and pans?

49. At the very start of *Five Go Down To The Sea*, how many minutes do the Five have to reach the train station in time: seven, twenty or forty?

50. In *Five On A Treasure Island*, what does the man planning to buy Kirrin Island want to build on it?

1. Who wields a huge sword to chase Mr Henning out of Finniston Farm?

2. Which character in *Five Are Together Again* turns out to be the thief who climbed the tower and stole the scientific papers?

3. When Berta is disguised as a boy, does she choose the name George, Lesley or Hilary?

4. What is the name of the girl who annoys George by acting like a boy in *Five Go To Mystery Moor*?

5. Do you open the mechanical gates to Owl Dene house by pulling a lever, pushing a knob behind the bookcase or turning a wheel?

6. Which of the Famous Five does the girl called Jo in *Five Fall Into Adventure* get on best with?

7. What fruit is Aunt Fanny picking when the Famous Five and the Lawdler twins arrive back at Kirrin Cottage: blackberries, pears, raspberries or cherries?

8. The secret sliding panel in Kirrin Cottage, found in the first Famous Five book, is in the middle of the top row of panels: true or false?

9. Is Wooden-Leg Sam a character in *Five On Kirrin Island Again*, *Five Go Off To Camp* or *Five Get Into A Fix*?

10. In *Five On Kirrin Island Again*, which member of the Famous Five does Uncle Quentin request to stay with him on the island?

11. Which of the Five puts on a diamond tiara and other pieces of the stolen jewellery found in *Five Go Off In A Caravan*?

12. Does Mr Luffy, Mr Andrews or Uncle Quentin tell the police about the missing children in the railway tunnel in *Five Go Off To Camp*?

13. Which two of these items does George buy from the general store in *Five Run Away Together*: torch batteries, a spade, some kindling wood, two boxes of matches?

14. Are the pages containing much of Uncle Quentin's secret formula found in a wooden chest, in a macintosh coat or in Timmy's kennel?

15. The first night that Mrs Stick doesn't serve the children supper, does Julian take jam tarts, blueberry muffins or gingerbread from the larder?

16. Does Red Tower live in a stone house on a cliff, in a caravan by the lake or in a shack in the middle of a wood?

17. Is Uncle Quentin, Mr Lenoir or Block gagged and taken out of Smuggler's Top through the catacombs?

18. In *Five Have Plenty Of Fun*, which girl wonders if her father would buy Kirrin Island, much to George's annoyance?

19. Which of the Five writes the note that is placed round Pongo's neck asking for help to be sent to the caves?

20. What relation to Enid Blyton was Sophie Smallwood, who wrote *Noddy And The Farmyard Muddle*, published to celebrate Noddy's 60th birthday?

21. What do the men who want to buy Old Towers want the rare metal buried in the hill for: to make jewellery, to power a new type of fuel station or to make bombs?

22. Sir James Lawton-Harrison is a very important scientist in which book: *Five On A Secret Trail*, *Five Fall Into Adventure* or *Five Are Together Again*?

23. Who points a gun at Timmy in *Five Go Off In A Caravan* and threatens to shoot him?

24. Who suggests that the Famous Five call their fourteenth adventure *Five Have Plenty Of Fun*: Aunt Fanny, Dick, George or Anne?

25. Julian and George take an injured Timmy to see someone said to be good with horses and other animals. Was it: Mr Gaston, Mr Perton, Mr Roland or Mr Jenkins?

26. In *Five On A Treasure Island*, does Anne, George or Dick pick up an old cup and half a saucer when they are exploring the shipwreck?

27. Is Mr Thomas, Mr Wilton or Mr Roland tall and thin with glasses perched on his nose?

28. In *Five Get Into A Fix*, how does Morgan get free of the ropes that bind his hands: he rubs them against a sharp rock, Dai the dog bites through them, or Anne cuts them with a penknife?

29. Can you recall the name of either of the farmhands who help the children escape from underground on Finniston Farm?

30. Does *Five Have A Mystery To Solve* start at Dick, Julian and Anne's house, Kirrin Cottage or at George and Anne's school?

31. Which of the following types of boat does not visit Kirrin Island in *Five On A Treasure Island:* a yacht, a rowing boat, a motorboat or a fishing smack?

32. In *Five Go To Demon's Rocks*, whose great-grandad is Jeremiah Boogle: Tinker Hayling's, Joanna's or Jackson the taxi-driver's?

33. Is Toby Thomas leading the Famous Five to blackberry bushes, a pool to swim in or a secret cave when they spot a 'Keep Out, Danger' warning sign?

34. Which one of the following is not at the riding school in *Five Go To Mystery Moor*: Alice, Susan, Claire or John?

35. In which book does Uncle Quentin agree to let George keep Timothy at home in Kirrin Cottage?

36. Does Lucas say a solid gold throne, a bed made of solid gold or a chest of gold coins was taken to the island in the harbour in *Five Have A Mystery To Solve*?

37. Which female cook tells George that Timmy is 'the nicest dog in the whole world' after he has given Mischief a ride on his back?

38. What do the Five find inside the tobacco pouch at Kirrin Farm: an iron key, a piece of linen, a gold brooch or a silver pendant?

39. Are the Five locked up in Tremannon Farm, an old castle, the hold of a ship or a cave in the cliffs during *Five Go Down To The Sea*?

40. In which book do the Famous Five encounter the acrobat and jewel thief whose full name is Lewis Allburg?

41. Does George, Aunt Fanny or Mr Roland have to stay in bed at Kirrin Cottage with a bad cold after Christmas in *Five Go Adventuring Again*?

42. In *Five Get Into Trouble*, does Richard kick Mr Perton, Rooky or Mr Weston hard in the ankles to escape to the police?

43. In *Five Go Off In A Caravan*, which of the Five manages to escape the caves and get help to save the others?

44. What treasure from the underground ruins of Finniston Castle do the twins show their parents?

45. What is the name of the Flight Lieutenant accused, along with Toby's cousin, of stealing aircraft?

46. In which book would you find a man who can weave himself in and out of the spokes of a caravan wheel?

47. George's great-great-great-grandfather's initials were H.J.K. What did the initals stand for?

48. Which two famous scientists disappear in *Five Have A Wonderful Time*: Thurlow Kent, Jeffrey Pottersham, Derek Terry-Kane, Victor Markhoff?

49. Does Mister India-rubber, Alfredo or Bufflo show the Famous Five where their caravans have been moved to?

50. Is Aunt Fanny cooking, cleaning or gardening when the Famous Five arrive home after escaping from Kirrin Island in *Five On A Treasure Island*?

QUIZ 19

1. Does Yan, Dick or Anne manage to slide the key under the door so that the Five can unlock it and escape from the cave in *Five Go Down To The Sea*?

2. Which member of the Famous Five nearly chokes to death on a ball in *Five Have A Mystery To Solve*?

3. Inside the treasure room on Whispering Island, what material are the beautiful stone animals carved from?

4. In which book are there two dogs called Dai: *Five Go Off To Camp*, *Five Get Into A Fix* or *Five Go To Mystery Moor*?

5. How do the Famous Five travel to Mystery Moor: on horseback, on their bicycles, using a horse and cart or on foot?

6. In *Five Go To Demon's Rocks*, do Julian and Dick gain access to the hidden treasure by entering the Wreckers' Cave, walking along the beach or going down through the foundations of the lighthouse?

7. As a child what name did Enid Blyton give to the stray kitten she kept secretly for two weeks as her mother didn't like pets: Timmy, Sooty, Chippy or Billy?

8. Who, along with Jeremiah and the village doctor, rows to Demon's Rocks lighthouse to rescue the Famous Five, Mischief and Tinker?

9. In *Five Go Off In A Caravan*, where are the circus men's stolen goods hidden: under the big top, in trees besides Merran Lake or in caves in the Merran Hills?

10. Which other member of the Famous Five stops George from sailing to Kirrin Island on her own to get away from Mr and Mrs Stick?

11. Is Mr Mackie the farmer's first name Lou, Ted, Bill or Reg?

12. Where are the two missing pilots in *Five Go To Billycock Hill* eventually found: on Kirrin Island, in Billycock Caves, locked in the butterfly farm or tied to a tree on Billycock Hill?

13. In *Five On A Treasure Island*, does the treasure map say the gold ingots are buried in the castle tower, its throne room or in the castle dungeons?

14. What animal does Timmy eat while he is kept in the tunnels in Castaway Hill: rabbits, spiders or rats?

15. Snippet the dog finds a historic item down a rabbit hole that the Five first think is a bone. Is it: a knight's helmet clasp, a jewelled hair pin or a dagger handle?

16. Do the Five travel to Kirrin Island, go to the police or go back to their schools when they see eighteen flashes given as a signal from Uncle Quentin's tower on Kirrin Island?

17. Are 'Good Luck', 'Bye for now' or 'Until the next time' the very last words of the last book in the Famous Five series?

18. Did Farmer Burrows, Mrs Andrews or Aunt Fanny give Jock Robins the collie dog when he was younger?

19. In *Five Get Into Trouble*, what outdoor present does Aunt Fanny buy Julian, Dick and Anne for Christmas?

20. Did Enid Blyton die in the 1950s, 1960s, 1970s or 1980s?

21. Mr Penruthlan says that Jenny is ill so he must go and look after her. Is Jenny his niece, a horse, his aunt or a cow?

22. In *Five Go Adventuring Again*, is there a handle, a book or a gold dagger behind the secret panel in Uncle Quentin's study?

23. At the end of the short story *Five Have A Puzzling Time*, is the light George sees on Kirrin Island actually: a reflection in the water, an aircraft flying above the island or a shooting star?

24. Madelon and her beautiful dancing horses are an act in which Famous Five book: *Five Have Plenty Of Fun*, *Five Go Off In A Caravan* or *Five Are Together Again*?

25. Who is the only adult in Kirrin Cottage when George is kidnapped in *Five Have Plenty Of Fun*?

26. Whose name does Sooty call out just before he is bumped on the head at Smuggler's Top: his mother's, Mr Barling's or Julian's?

27. Who climbs down the well to rescue George and Julian from the Kirrin Castle dungeons?

28. When Berta goes back to being a girl again after being disguised as a boy, what girl's name does she adopt: Brenda, Jane, Carrie or Petra?

29. How do the fair folk trap Uncle Quentin: do they tie him up and put him in a caravan, handcuff him to the stables or lock him in a box with snakes?

30. Which boy gets scared on Kirrin Island and thinks cows are throwing things at him?

31. On their first night away in *Five Get Into Trouble,* do the Famous Five sleep in their tents, at a farmhouse or out in the open?

32. Where does George take Timmy to camp at the start of *Five On A Secret Trail*: on the local common, on Kirrin Island or just outside the village of Great Giddings?

33. Does Meg's gran tell the Famous Five about Two-Trees in *Five On A Hike Together*, *Five Get Into Trouble* or *Five Fall Into Adventure*?

34. How does Guy Lawdler travel from the camp to Kirrin Cottage: by bus, using George's bicycle, on a horse or by taxi?

35. Does Aily, her dog, her lamb or all three of them hide in the top bunk bed in the mountainside hut when Morgan arrives?

36. Do the Famous Five search the artists' bedrooms, the kitchen or the lounge and study of Kirrin Farmhouse to try and find the pages of Uncle Quentin's stolen formula?

37. How many pages of the book Uncle Quentin is working on in *Five Go Adventuring Again* are stolen when the test tubes in his study are broken?

38. What is the first name of Mrs Stick, the new housekeeper at Kirrin Cottage: Clara, Sarah or Jennifer?

39. What name does Ben the blacksmith say Mystery Moor used to be known by?

40. What is the first village where the Famous Five stop and have ice creams when they set off by bike in *Five Go To Billycock Hill*: Tennick, Great Giddings or Mablethorpe?

41. In *Five Go Off In A Caravan*, are Julian, Dick and Anne's parents heading abroad, up north or staying at home when the children go on holiday?

42. In *Five Run Away Together*, who hides the key to their store cupboard in their dressing table?

43. Which character in *Five Have A Mystery To Solve* was, in the past, a keeper on the mysterious Whispering Island: Lucas, Wilfrid or Mrs Layman?

44. Were *The Magic Faraway Tree*, *Adventures Of The Wishing Chair* and *The Land Of Far-Beyond* all children's books written by Enid Blyton?

45. What item, normally found on clothing, do the Famous Five find inside the large sea chest which has the name Abram Trelawny painted on it?

46. Is one of the men who imprison George and Julian on Kirrin Island called James, Roger, Jake or Gregory?

47. In *Five On A Treasure Island*, what does George use to open the locked cupboard in the captain's quarters of the shipwreck?

48. Are the two artists staying with Mr and Mrs Sanders at Kirrin Farm for a weekend, one week or three weeks?

49. What does Mr Thomas the farmer insist Julian and the others take to help find their way back from Billycock Caves: chalk to make marks, a compass or a ball of string?

50. In which book does Timmy get drugged for days as he and George are held prisoner: *Five Go Down To The Sea*, *Five Fall Into Adventure* or *Five Get Into A Fix*?

Tough Questions

1. In the short story *Five Have A Puzzling Time*, who loses a sandal on Kirrin Island?

2. Who throws the stone that strikes Pongo on the head and knocks him out?

3. What is the name of Tinker's small boat, moored close to Demon's Rocks lighthouse?

4. In which book does Dick call Anne a mouse and Julian call George a tiger in the same conversation?

5. Who hung a school bully up on a coat peg for bullying a small boy?

6. Which man argues with old Great-grandad at Finniston Farm and criticises England as 'poor' and 'run-down'?

7. How many children are staying at Captain Johnson's Riding School, including Dick and Julian?

8. Who knocks out Sooty and takes him and Uncle Quentin into the catacombs of Castaway Hill?

9. What is the name of the escaped prisoner kept in Owl's Dene by Mr Perton and Rooky?

10. Can you name the long lane between Kirrin and where the Famous Five camped in *Five On A Secret Trail*?

11. What two words were printed on the top of the linen map found at Kirrin Farm in *Five Go Adventuring Again*?

12. In which book do the Famous Five go cycling, meet the son of one of the richest men in Britain and discover an escaped prisoner?

13. Who lays secret messages on the ground for the Famous Five to follow the travellers' caravans on to Mystery Moor?

14. What is the name of the female acrobat from the fair in Faynights Field?

15. In the short story *Well Done, Famous Five!*, who owns the racehorses that the children see being exercised?

16. What is the name of the horse that pulls the caravan in which Jo and her father live?

17. In *Five Go Off In A Caravan*, how many times bigger than a dance hall do the Famous Five estimate the cavern is?

18. When hiring a boat in *Five Have A Mystery To Solve*, how much is Julian told it will cost for a day?

19. When stopping for fifteen minutes on the way to Magga Glen, how many crumpets do the Famous Five eat between them?

20. What is the name of the scientist Uncle Quentin is working with in the short story, *Good Old Timmy!*?

21. Who calls the electric fence around Old Towers 'the fence that bites'?

22. On Whispering Island, what item of food does Timmy steal and bring back to Dick, Julian, George and Anne?

23. Who does Bobby Loman live with: his Granpop, his mother, Joanna the cook or at an orphanage?

24. What is the name of the town, starting with the letter E, that Mr Andrews drives Jock Robins to in order to keep him away from the Famous Five?

25. Who hit Dick on the jaw near the start of *Five Fall Into Adventure*?

26. What was the name of Peter and Janet's dog in Enid Blyton's *Secret Seven* series?

27. In *Five On A Secret Trail*, what size shoes does Dick reckon made the footprints outside the ruined cottage window?

28. What tune is played at the end of the Barnies' show, in *Five Go Down To The Sea*?

29. In *Five On A Hike Together*, what is the name of Jim's brother who is a warder at the local prison?

30. Who drives the Famous Five to the police station at Gathercombe so they can hand over the stolen jewellery?

31. What was the name of the inn found in Beacons?

32. In *Five Get Into A Fix*, who is Morgan Jones's life-long enemy?

33. What are the three digits of the telephone number for Kirrin Cottage?

34. In the short story *George's Hair Is Too Long*, to which cove are the Five heading, stopping in the village on the way?

35. What is the telephone number of the doctor in Kirrin: 018, 042, 179 or 236?

36. Which two men lock the Five in the Demon's Rocks lighthouse so that they can find the old wreckers' treasure?

37. In the short story *Well Done, Famous Five!*, what is the name of the racehorse that Julian says is the most valuable in the whole country?

38. In *Five Go To Mystery Moor*, what is the name of the secret traveller messages made out of patterns of sticks, leaves and stones?

39. In *Five Are Together Again*, what is the name of the field next to Professor Hayling and Tinker's house?

40. Can you recall the first six words of the strange message Dick receives from Nailer in *Five On A Hike Together*?

41. Which island did Enid Blyton visit on her honeymoon which would later inspire Kirrin Island in the Famous Five series?

42. What is the registration plate of the black car in *Five Get Into Trouble*?

43. In Enid Blyton's Noddy books, which mischievous character appears to be half monkey and half bunny rabbit?

44. What do the Five find on the stone steps of the tower used by the wreckers that proves someone has been there recently?

45. In the short story *Five And A Half-Term Adventure*, where do the Famous Five catch the train from to return to Kirrin?

46. What is the name of the bad boy from Kirrin who attempts to steal the Famous Five's sack of Christmas presents?

47. What is the name of the fishing boat that George hides the scientific papers in before rowing to Kirrin Island?

48. In the Famous Five series, who invents the electric trosymon?

49. To what place, beginning with P, did Dick, Julian, Anne and their parents usually go on holiday?

50. Which scientist do the Famous Five find in a room at the top of the tower of Faynights Castle?

Answers

Note: the questions and answers in this book are taken from the 'classic' editions of the *Famous Five* titles.

1. Georgina (George)
2. One
3. 21
4. Julian
5. *Five On A Treasure Island*
6. Dick
7. Noddy
8. Kirrin Island
9. George
10. Fanny

11. Anne
12. Timothy (Timmy)
13. True
14. The blue caravan
15. Quentin
16. Two
17. Brown
18. Two
19. False
20. Anne's mother

21. An elephant
22. Her father
23. Rabbits
24. Anne
25. George

26. They camp in a field
27. Socks
28. A scientist
29. Her mother
30. Junior

31. George's father
32. Dick
33. Kirrin Cottage
34. 1897
35. A teacher at Dick and Julian's school
36. George
37. George and Timmy
38. Clopper
39. The boys' train
40. Short and bearded

41. Julian
42. Anne
43. Joanna
44. Not waterproof
45. False
46. George
47. A shipwreck
48. Uncle Quentin
49. True
50. George

QUIZ 1

1. Julian
2. 25p
3. Big Hollow
4. Yes
5. Wales
6. A ruined castle
7. A poem
8. George
9. Gringo
10. *Five Go To Mystery Moor*

11. *Five On Finniston Farm*
12. Jet
13. Mrs Layman
14. Junior
15. Uncle Quentin
16. Mr Luffy
17. Dick
18. The Green Pool
19. George
20. *Adventure*

21. Mr Brent
22. Julian
23. A sailor
24. Timmy
25. *Five Go To Mystery Moor*
26. Harriet
27. George
28. Trotter
29. *Five Go To Demon's Rocks*
30. Julian

31. Bufflo
32. A monkey
33. Four
34. Scarlet fever
35. Henrietta

36. Her father fears she might be kidnapped
37. Toby
38. August
39. George
40. A snake

41. Chalk
42. Edgar
43. Oliver
44. Lunch
45. Mr Gaston
46. One-Ear Bill
47. Sniffer's father
48. Timmy
49. Aily
50. Lacrosse

QUIZ 2

1. Anne
2. Twelve years old
3. London
4. Timmy
5. *Five Have A Wonderful Time*
6. Liz
7. Nobby
8. Two
9. A pony trap
10. Her father's study

11. A dog
12. *Five Get Into Trouble*
13. Tremannon
14. Wilfrid
15. George and Timmy
16. Uncle Quentin
17. Cuddles
18. The attic
19. April

20. A spade
21. Miss Peters
22. An old-fashioned hat
23. Guy Lawdler
24. Timmy
25. Berta
26. Money (banknotes)
27. Julian
28. Dacca
29. Mr Tapper
30. Cars

31. Stepfather
32. Mischief
33. Richard Kent
34. A helicopter
35. Three
36. Benny
37. Old Towers
38. A caravan
39. Johnson
40. Red

41. *Merry Meg*
42. George
43. Cricket
44. Wooden-Leg Sam
45. The Guv'nor
46. Edgar
47. Timmy
48. Husband
49. The United States of America
50. Curly

QUIZ 3

1. Dick
2. A circus procession
3. Philpot
4. Uncle Quentin

5. Mary
6. April
7. Blue eyes
8. The Alphabet game
9. Two
10. The Sanders

11. Summer
12. A farmer
13. George
14. Captain Johnson's Riding School
15. Sand
16. A joke spider
17. Paul
18. A real person
19. A spiral staircase
20. France

21. Great Giddings
22. George
23. Dick
24. A good swimmer
25. A cruise
26. Red
27. His leg
28. Red
29. A portable radio
30. A fiddle player

31. Julian
32. An ash tree
33. Wilfrid
34. By car
35. Moth
36. Jim and Stan
37. A donkey
38. The sound of an aeroplane
39. Mrs Thomas
40. George

41. High Cliffs
42. Tinker
43. Gaylands
44. Timmy
45. Anne
46. 1952
47. A fire eater
48. France
49. *Five Run Away Together*
50. Edgar Stick

QUIZ 4

1. Dick
2. Marshes
3. A very fast driver
4. A rowing boat
5. *Five Go Off To Camp*
6. October
7. Jackdaws
8. Sniffer
9. Markhoff
10. Aggie

11. George
12. Buns
13. Toby
14. *Five Go To Smuggler's Top*
15. Barling
16. A leg
17. Three
18. November
19. Uncle Dan
20. Timmy

21. Bats
22. Cornwall
23. Milling Green
24. Jo
25. In a bookcase

26. Skippy
27. Fallaway Hill
28. Henry
29. James
30. Canaries

31. A lighthouse
32. Dangerous drugs
33. One week
34. Joanna
35. Hill Cottage
36. Dick and George
37. Jenny
38. Tinker
39. Seven
40. A cook

41. Anne's
42. Four miles
43. Mary
44. Wales
45. Dick
46. Bill
47. Anne
48. Old Lady
49. Heather
50. They crash into the sea

QUIZ 5

1. George
2. France
3. Mr Luffy
4. Red
5. Jo
6. Radio transmitter
7. A chimpanzee
8. George
9. Harry
10. Amanda

11. Uncle Quentin
12. *Five Are Together Again*
13. Wilfrid
14. At home
15. Collies
16. Jackdaws
17. Spain
18. George
19. Aunt Fanny
20. Younger

21. *Cheeky Charlie*
22. Snap
23. Richard Kent
24. Dirty Dick
25. Mischief the monkey
26. Tobogganing
27. Cutlery
28. Morgan
29. Plums
30. Jim

31. Scientists
32. Leg
33. Anne
34. Old Towers
35. An ironmongers shop
36. An air force pilot
37. By boat
38. Stew
39. Tea
40. London

41. Growler, Barker
42. Hot cocoa
43. Sweets
44. Wreckers
45. Mischief
46. Timmy
47. Three hours
48. Beauty

49. Dick
50. Timmy

QUIZ 6

1. 35 miles per hour
2. Dobby
3. Professor Hayling's
4. Ten years
5. She wrote out her books by hand
6. Gringo's Great Fair
7. Edith Wells
8. The Bartle family
9. Julian
10. A monkey

11. Fifteen children
12. Blue
13. Aunt Fanny
14. An Alsatian
15. Car
16. *Five Go Off In A Caravan*
17. Barker
18. Martin
19. A new way of generating power
20. Anne

21. £10.00
22. Jake
23. Carey
24. Scotland
25. Spitting a damson stone
26. No
27. Gloomy Water
28. *Five Have A Wonderful Time*
29. 5p
30. He doesn't put his false teeth in

31. *Noddy And The Aeroplane*
32. Journalist
33. Easter holidays
34. Uncle Dan
35. Eight
36. They vanished on the moor
37. Anne
38. Anne and George
39. Dick
40. They tell them to clear off and leave the field

41. Ravens Wood
42. Martin
43. Poodle
44. Oak Tree Pond
45. Using a spiral staircase
46. Mr Wooh
47. *Five Get Into A Fix*
48. A Roman coin
49. A baby hedgehog
50. Policemen

QUIZ 7

1. Julian
2. 1192
3. Spiky
4. The tower
5. Helena Bonham Carter
6. Her hip
7. The Lenoir family cook
8. Go back to school
9. Tuesday
10. Kirrin

11. Yellow and blue
12. Uncle Quentin
13. Manlington-Tovey
14. Monkeys

15. Dick
16. The Inspector
17. Julian
18. Ben, Willy, Nellie, Bouncer
19. Dick
20. Tapper's Travelling Circus

21. London Zoo
22. Dog biscuits, orange peel
23. By parachute
24. Edgar's
25. April
26. In his kennel
27. Their toboggans
28. Olly's Farm
29. George and Timmy
30. Dick

31. A python
32. Mr Penruthlan
33. Henrietta
34. They hear it on the radio
35. Uncle Quentin
36. Six macaroons
37. Millie
38. Hannah and Lucy
39. A collie
40. Bentley

41. Aily
42. Cocoa
43. *Five On A Hike Together*
44. Elbur
45. Peters
46. Sheep
47. Orangeade
48. Peter
49. Green
50. Julian

QUIZ 8

1. Charlie
2. Block
3. 20 miles
4. Julian
5. Dai
6. Gold statues
7. Dick and Toby
8. Insects
9. The Secret series
10. 569

11. A monkey
12. A chocolate ice-cream bar
13. Huge meals
14. A cave
15. Coal
16. Sweets
17. Jenny
18. Nobby
19. A glass room
20. Biddy

21. Anne
22. *Merry Meg*
23. A laundry basket
24. Yan
25. A surgeon
26. September
27. A diary
28. By phoning the police from the Mackies' farm
29. £4,000
30. The attic

31. An ex-acrobat
32. Aunt Fanny
33. Kirrin Cottage
34. A large brass bell
35. Anne

36. Dirty Dick
37. A train track
38. Two days
39. Toby
40. Mashed potatoes

41. Morgan
42. Guy Lawdler
43. Black
44. The post office
45. Ebenezer, Jacob
46. Henrietta
47. None, she is an only child
48. An iron door halfway down
49. *Saucy Jane*
50. The Harries (Henry and Harriet Philpot)

QUIZ 9

1. George
2. Edgar
3. Four
4. The shoulder
5. Lake Merran
6. Timmy
7. George
8. The Three Wreckers
9. George
10. Sydney

11. Chippy
12. Sid
13. She cannot read or write
14. Ginger buns
15. 'Red Tower'
16. A bicycle
17. Anne
18. Pierre Lenoir
19. Longman's Farm
20. A travel clock

21. Dick
22. Mrs Andrews
23. Rooky
24. Mr Wilton
25. The Sticks
26. Willis and Johnson
27. A raft
28. Pickled onions
29. Limming Ho
30. The funnel of the old train engine

31. 1942
32. Llewellyn
33. Lou
34. Block
35. The Guv'nor
36. George's dressing gown
37. Father
38. Some barbed wire
39. Stealing ducks
40. Anita

41. Mr Curton
42. Morgan's
43. Suits of armour
44. Tea-sup
45. Joanna the cook
46. Four
47. Timmy
48. A.A. Milne
49. Mr Roland
50. Tinker

QUIZ 10

1. Jet
2. A whip-cracker
3. Wailing Island, Whispering Island

4. Dorset
5. 6 o'clock
6. Diamonds
7. Mrs Janes
8. By taxi
9. Anne
10. Cricket

11. George
12. Mr Penruthlan
13. By car
14. Three
15. Black
16. A gorse bush
17. Geometry
18. The Bonzo Band
19. Julian
20. Yan

21. Larry
22. The shepherd
23. Cheddar
24. *Five On A Secret Trail*
25. 10.30
26. Harriet
27. Perry
28. Dick
29. Block
30. Measles

31. 60 parcels
32. The Royal Air Force
33. George
34. St Clare's
35. Dick
36. On Christmas Eve
37. Hunchy
38. A torch
39. *Dab*
40. Julian

41. A railway timetable
42. Seven
43. The Barnies
44. Timmy
45. A ball of string
46. *Five Go Adventuring Again*
47. Six
48. Boxes of valuable goods
49. Twining
50. A snow-slide

QUIZ 11

1. Timmy
2. Castaway Hill
3. Holland
4. A rabbit hole
5. True
6. Dick
7. Joanna
8. Martin
9. Mr Roland
10. Over eighty years old

11. George
12. Tinky
13. Delivering newspapers
14. Monty and Winks
15. Berta
16. The coastguard
17. Ebenezer
18. Ivor
19. Pippin
20. America

21. Aunt Fanny
22. The piano
23. Two
24. His tail
25. Twice a day

26. Uncle Alfredo
27. A sword and a dagger
28. Mr Wooh
29. Tom, Jess, Paul
30. Kirrin Cottage

31. Kiki
32. A windmill
33. Timmy
34. Morgan
35. *Robin Hood*
36. The ruined castle on Kirrin Island
37. Pierre Lenoir
38. Anne
39. Betsy-May
40. A peg rope

41. Planks and heather
42. Dick
43. Trippers
44. Older
45. Jewellery
46. Dick
47. John
48. A table-tennis table
49. Julian
50. Mrs Janes

QUIZ 12

1. *Child Whispers*
2. A chocolate cake
3. Aladdin
4. Cricket
5. Rummy
6. *Five On A Treasure Island*
7. A gun
8. Anne
9. His ankle
10. Dick

11. *Five Go Down To The Sea*
12. None
13. Henry
14. Fany
15. Seven
16. Julian
17. Three weeks
18. Guy Lawdler
19. Second flight
20. Jeffrey Pottersham

21. Owl Hill
22. Sally
23. Blue
24. A black poodle
25. Flight-lieutenant
26. George
27. Dick and Julian
28. £1.00
29. Anne
30. Joanna

31. Jo
32. Spiggy House
33. Henrietta
34. Julian
35. William Finniston
36. A butterfly
37. Green
38. The Ministry of Research
39. A motorcycle
40. George

41. On Merren Hills
42. Mr Lenoir's
43. An American scientist
44. *The Roamer*
45. Fifty pence
46. Block

47. The railway porter at Kirrin Station
48. The two boys
49. Fury
50. Red Tower

QUIZ 13

1. Dick's
2. Explorer
3. On Kirrin Island
4. Dr Drew
5. The Normans
6. Bryn
7. *The Five Find-Outers*
8. Tom
9. False
10. Jo's hand

11. *Five Go To Smuggler's Top*
12. Harry Armstrong
13. On the golf course
14. A baby hedgehog
15. Professor Hayling
16. His new pocket knife
17. A robbery
18. Benny
19. A Brown Argus
20. The coal hole

21. His travelling clock
22. A caravan
23. A radio
24. Simmy, Jake, Red
25. A pear tree
26. George
27. Richard
28. Timmy
29. George
30. Block

31. An axe
32. Dick and Julian
33. Lily
34. A rabbit
35. Dick
36. Nobby's father
37. Hunchy
38. George
39. A dog
40. An artist

41. Dobby
42. Tremannon Farm
43. Anne
44. Artist
45. Alfredo
46. Anne's
47. Someone escaping from the prison
48. Bananas in Pyjamas
49. A secret formula
50. American dollars

QUIZ 14

1. Gringo
2. A teacher
3. Red
4. Little
5. Aggie
6. Anne
7. *Five Run Away Together*
8. A new collar
9. North
10. Anne

11. *Daily Clarion*
12. *The Secret Garden*
13. Sally
14. Barney Boswell

15. Kirrin Farmhouse
16. Mr Lenoir
17. Edgar Stick
18. Dick and Julian
19. His cousin (Jeff)
20. Tiger Dan and Lou

21. The henhouse
22. Mr Wooh
23. Martin
24. An ice cream
25. Tock Hill
26. Dick
27. Julian
28. Curly the pig
29. Blue
30. Gringo

31. Playing soldiers
32. A brown leather bag
33. A flight in a plane
34. George
35. Mr Durleston
36. Anne
37. Plums
38. Julian
39. A shepherd
40. A jackdaw bird

41. His whistle
42. £15.00
43. *Five On A Hike Together*
44. Three
45. Paraffin oil
46. Archaeology
47. Bacon and eggs
48. Jock
49. An underground metal mine
50. Demon's Rocks lighthouse

QUIZ 15

1. A dog trainer
2. Six
3. *Saucy Sue*
4. A grain store
5. George
6. Jackdaws
7. London
8. Mr Slither, Mister India-rubber, Alfredo and Bufflo
9. George and Timmy
10. Three

11. Eleven
12. Hunchy
13. Seville
14. A storm
15. His stepfather
16. Mr Curton
17. A garage
18. George
19. Wine cellars
20. Emilio, Carlo

21. Marybelle
22. The head of the horse costume
23. France
24. Anne and George
25. A shepherd
26. After Christmas Day
27. Harry Lawdler
28. Red
29. £100,000
30. Lucilla

31. Four years
32. 'Secret Way'
33. Blue Pond Farm
34. Sooty

35. Three
36. Malory Towers series
37. Owl Farm
38. Eggs, bacon and sausages
39. Smuggler's Top
40. Bufflo's knife

41. Ben and Fred
42. Two
43. Dick's
44. Ancient Roman
45. Oliver Cromwell
46. Over 60 years old
47. Dick and Julian
48. Benny
49. Police Constable Sharp
50. Joanna

QUIZ 16

1. His pyjamas
2. Ginger beer
3. Lomax
4. Berta
5. James
6. The kitchen
7. Julian and Dick
8. Anita
9. A revolver gun
10. Monopoly

11. Jeremiah Boogle
12. A snake
13. Harry Lawdler
14. Anne
15. *Five Have A Puzzling Time*
16. Caves
17. Two
18. Tinker
19. Timmy
20. Children's clothes

21. Ham sandwiches
22. Mr Binks
23. The cinema
24. Dick
25. £100,000
26. Jo
27. Timmy
28. Down in the quarry
29. His shoulder
30. Crowleg Vale

31. Bread and honey
32. George
33. It is washed away by a strong tide
34. Over the cliffs
35. Eight
36. Jacob Loomer's
37. 'Chimney'
38. George
39. Mr Roland
40. The old quarry

41. The castle dungeons
42. £5,000
43. Mrs Stick
44. Timmy
45. Whooping cough
46. Timmy
47. Green
48. A statue of an angel
49. Tiger Dan
50. Thurlow Kent

QUIZ 17

1. True
2. Mr Lenoir
3. Uncle Quentin
4. Twelve and blond-haired
5. Breakfast

6. Fourteen
7. Peter, Janet, Barbara, Pam, George, Jack and Colin
8. Anne
9. An ironmongers
10. Julian

11. Alf
12. The Green Pool
13. The fishermen
14. Timmy
15. Dai, Tang, Bob
16. Jo
17. His parents
18. Timmy
19. William and Henrietta
20. Mary Pollock

21. £100,000
22. Alf
23. In a shed in a field
24. Blue and green
25. To see the sea and talk to fishermen
26. Julian
27. Mr Jenkins
28. A book of recipes
29. Biscuit, Bonzo, Brownie, Bones, Bunter
30. Armstrong

31. Six loaves
32. A notebook
33. Keep-Away Island
34. Will Janes
35. Jim
36. Gold bars
37. Dick
38. Dirty Dick and Maggie
39. The travellers
40. Mr Penruthlan

41. Mr Andrews, Mr Peters
42. On the roof
43. The Wreckers' Way
44. On skis
45. Junior Henning
46. Toby
47. Uncle Quentin
48. A brass cannon
49. Seven minutes
50. A hotel

QUIZ 18

1. Great-grandad
2. Charlie the chimpanzee
3. Lesley
4. Henrietta (Henry)
5. Turning a wheel
6. Dick
7. Raspberries
8. True
9. *Five Go Off To Camp*
10. Timmy

11. Anne
12. Mr Luffy
13. Torch batteries, two boxes of matches
14. In a macintosh coat
15. Jam tarts
16. In a stone house on a cliff
17. Uncle Quentin
18. Berta
19. Dick
20. Her granddaughter

21. To make bombs
22. *Five On A Secret Trail*
23. Lou
24. George

25. Mr Gaston
26. Anne
27. Mr Thomas
28. Dai the dog bites through them
29. Jamie, Bill
30. Dick, Julian and Anne's house

31. A yacht
32. Jackson the taxi driver's
33. A pool to swim in
34. Claire
35. *Five On A Treasure Island*
36. A bed made of solid gold
37. Joanna
38. A piece of linen
39. A cave in the cliffs
40. *Five Go Off In A Caravan*

41. Mr Roland
42. Mr Perton
43. Dick
44. Gold coins
45. Ray Wells
46. *Five Have A Wonderful Time*
47. Henry John Kirrin
48. Jeffrey Pottersham, Derek Terry-Kane
49. Mister India-rubber
50. Gardening

QUIZ 19

1. Yan
2. Timmy
3. Jade
4. *Five Get Into A Fix*
5. On horseback
6. Going down through

the foundations of the
lighthouse

7. Chippy
8. Police Constable Sharp
9. In caves in the Merran Hills
10. Julian

11. Ted
12. In Billycock Caves
13. In the castle dungeons
14. Rats
15. A dagger handle
16. Travel to Kirrin Island
17. 'Good Luck'
18. Farmer Burrows
19. Two small tents
20. 1960s (1968)

21. A horse
22. A handle
23. A shooting star
24. *Five Are Together Again*
25. Joanna
26. Mr Barling's
27. Dick
28. Jane

29. Tie him up and put him in
a caravan
30. Edgar Stick

31. Out in the open
32. On the local common
33. *Five On A Hike Together*
34. Using George's bicycle
35. All three of them
36. The artists' bedrooms
37. Three
38. Clara
39. Misty Moor
40. Tennick

41. Heading up north
42. Aunt Fanny
43. Lucas
44. Yes
45. A button
46. Jake
47. A pocket knife
48. Three weeks
49. A ball of string
50. *Five Fall Into Adventure*

1. Anne
2. Tiger Dan
3. *Bob-About*
4. *Five Have A Mystery To Solve*
5. Mr Luffy
6. Mr Henning
7. Ten
8. Mr Barling
9. Solomon Weston
10. Carter's Lane

11. Via occulta
12. *Five Get Into Trouble*
13. Sniffer
14. Pearl
15. Lord Daniron
16. Blackie
17. Six times
18. £6.00
19. Nine (two for each of the four children and one for Timmy)
20. Professor Humes

21. Aily
22. A ham
23. His Granpop
24. Endersfield

25. Jo
26. Scamper
27. Size 8
28. God Save The Queen
29. Tom
30. Mr Gaston

31. The Three Shepherds
32. Llewellyn Thomas
33. 011
34. Windy Cove
35. 042
36. Ebenezer and Jacob
37. Thunder-Along
38. Patrins
39. Cromwell's Corner
40. Two-Trees Gloomy Water Saucy Jane

41. Jersey
42. KMF 102
43. The Bunkey
44. Oil stains
45. Beckton
46. Tom
47. *Gypsy*
48. Professor Hayling
49. Polseath
50. Derek Terry-Kane

More classic stories from the world of

Enid Blyton

The Famous Five Colour Short Stories

Enid Blyton also wrote eight short stories about the
Famous Five. Here they are, in their original texts,
with brand-new illustrations. They're a perfect
introduction to the gang, and an exciting new way to
enjoy classic Blyton stories.

More classic stories from the world of

Enid Blyton

Enid Blyton's Adventure Treasury

A must for Blyton fans, this beautiful giftbook is a
collection of her most exciting writing. Join many of
her best-loved heroes as they solve mysteries,
explore new places and foil baddies!

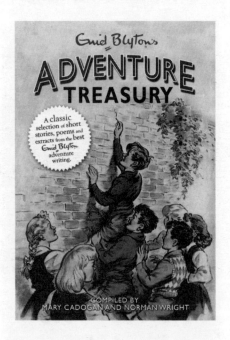

More classic stories from the world of

Enid Blyton

The Naughtiest Girl

Elizabeth Allen is spoilt and selfish. When's she's sent away to boarding school she makes up her mind to be the naughtiest pupil there's ever been! But Elizabeth soon finds out that being bad isn't as simple as it seems. There are ten brilliant books about the Naughtiest Girl to enjoy.

More classic stories from the world of

Enid Blyton

The Secret Seven

Join Peter, Janet, Jack, Barbara, Pam, Colin, George and Scamper as they solve puzzles and mysteries, foil baddies, and rescue people from danger – all without help from the grown-ups. Enid Blyton wrote fifteen stories about the Secret Seven. These editions contain brilliant illustrations by Tony Ross, plus extra fun facts and stories to read and share.